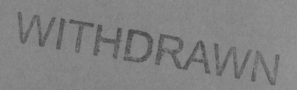

JOYCE CAROL OATES

MODERN LITERATURE MONOGRAPHS

GENERAL EDITOR: Lina Mainiero

In the same series:

(continued on last page of book)

JOYCE CAROL OATES

Ellen G. Friedman

FREDERICK UNGAR PUBLISHING CO.
NEW YORK

Copyright © 1980 by Frederick Ungar Publishing Co., Inc.
Printed in the United States of America
Design by Anita Duncan

Library of Congress Cataloging in Publication Data

Friedman, Ellen G   1944-
  Joyce Carol Oates.

  (Modern literature monographs)
  Bibliography: p.
  Includes index.
  1. Oates, Joyce Carol, 1938-   —Criticism and
interpretation.
  PS3565.A8Z65   813'.5'4   79-4828
  ISBN 0-8044-2221-4

The author acknowledges the kind permission of Joyce
Carol Oates to quote from her works for this study. The
copyright in the quoted text remains with Oates.

For Max, Sonia, and Rebecca

Contents

Chronology

1938　Joyce Carol Oates born to Caroline and Frederic Oates on June 16 in Millerport, New York.

1956　Awarded scholarship to Syracuse University.

1960　Graduates Phi Beta Kappa from Syracuse University with B.A. in English. Valedictorian of class.

1961　Marries Raymond J. Smith, Jr., on January 23. Earns M.A. in English from University of Wisconsin. Begins doctoral studies at Rice University. One of her stories appears on the Honor Roll in Martha Foley's *The Best American Short Stories*. The discovery of her story on the Honor Roll encourages her to stop her formal studies in order to write.

1962　Appointed Instructor in English, University of Detroit.

1963　*By the North Gate* is published.

1964　*With Shuddering Fall* is published.

1966　*Upon the Sweeping Flood* is published.

1967　*A Garden of Earthly Delights* is published. Accepts position of Assistant Professor of English, University of Windsor. Wins O. Henry Prize Award, First Prize. Awarded a Guggenheim Fellowship.

1968　*Expensive People* is published. *Women in Love and Other Poems* is published. Awarded the Richard and Hinda Rosenthal Award of the National Institute of Arts and Letters.

1969　*them* is published. *Anonymous Sins and Other Poems* is published.

1970   *The Wheel of Love and Other Stories* is published.
       Love and Its Derangements and Other Poems is
       published. Wins the National Book Award for *them*.
       Receives Special Award for Continuing Achieve-
       ment in connection with the O. Henry Prize Awards.

1971   *Wonderland* is published.

1972   *Marriages and Infidelities* is published. *The Edge
       of Impossibility: Tragic Forms in Literature* is pub-
       lished. Edits *Scenes from American Life: Contem-
       porary Short Fiction.*

1973   *Do With Me What You Will* is published. *Wonder-
       land* (revised edition) is published. *Angel Fire* is
       published. *Dreaming America* is published.

1974   *The Goddess and Other Women* is published. *The
       Hungry Ghosts: Seven Allusive Comedies* is pub-
       lished. *Where Are You Going, Where Have You
       Been?: Stories of Young America* is published. *Mir-
       acle Play* is published. *New Heaven, New Earth:
       The Visionary Experience in Literature* is pub-
       lished. With Raymond J. Smith, begins publishing
       *The Ontario Review: A North American Journal of
       the Arts.*

1975   *The Assassins: A Book of Hours* is published. *The
       Poisoned Kiss and Other Stories* is published. *The
       Seduction and Other Stories* is published. *The Fab-
       ulous Beasts* is published. Awarded the Lotos Club
       Award of Merit.

1976   *Childwold* is published. *The Triumph of the Spider
       Monkey: The First Person Confession of the Maniac
       Bobby Gotteson as Told to Joyce Carol Oates* is
       published. *Crossing the Border: Fifteen Tales* is
       published.

1977   *Night-Side: Eighteen Tales* is published.

1978   *Son of the Morning* is published. *All the Good Peo-
       ple I've Left Behind* is published. *Women Whose
       Lives Are Food, Men Whose Lives Are Money* is
       published. Appointed Writer-in-Residence at Prin-
       ceton University. Elected to the American Academy
       and Institute of Arts and Letters. Invited to be Guest
       Editor of the 1979 edition of *The Best American
       Short Stories.*

1

Variation
on an American Hymn

After meditating on the life and works of Joyce Carol
Oates, critics have sometimes felt compelled to
comment on the apparent incongruity of her life,
which she herself defines as ordinary, even "bour-
geois," and her fiction, which is filled with violent
episodes.[1] In an interview with Oates, Walter Clemons writes, "She is so gentle that if you met her
at a literary party and failed to catch her name, it
might be hard to imagine her reading, much less
writing, the unflinching fiction of Joyce Carol
Oates."[2] She has been described by reviewers as
"crowded with psychic existences," as having "violence in the head," and as the fourth Brontë sister."[3]
"Typical activities in Oates's novels," says one reviewer, "are arson, rape, riot, mental breakdown,
murder (plain and fancy, with excursions into pa-
tricide, matricide, uxoricide, mass filicide), and suicide,"[4] To read Oates, says another reviewer, "is
to cross an emotional minefield, to be stunned to
the soul by multiple explosions . . . ."[5]

Joyce Carol Oates describes her own nature as
"orderly and observant and scrupulous, and deeply
introverted,"[6] In interviews and at poetry readings,
she speaks with satisfaction of her "ordinary" life
and with nostalgia of her childhood. Since 1961 she
has been married to Raymond J. Smith, Jr., whom

she met at the University of Wisconsin where she earned a Master's degree in English. They have both taught at the University of Windsor since 1967.

In her fiction, Oates often returns to the rural landscapes of her childhood. The "Eden County" of many of her stories and novels represents the environs of Millerport in upstate New York where she grew up. She describes the Millerport of her childhood as a place where few people went to school beyond the seventh grade. Oates did, in fact, attend a one-room schoolhouse, and she was the first in her family to go to college. Her parents—religious, working class Catholics—were deeply affected by the Depression, a central symbol of dislocation in Oates's fiction. Her parents had to stop school at an early age in order to earn money. Her father became a tool and die designer, and her grandfather of whose death she speaks with deep regret and who may have inspired the portrait of the grandfather in *Childwold,* was a steelworker.[7] In explaining why a number of her novels begin in the 1930's, the decade of her birth, Oates says, "This was the world of my parents, who were young at the time . . . . I identify closely with my parents."[8]

Indeed, despite the violent dislocations her characters suffer, Oates places great emphasis on their family ties. The central characters of her novels have grandparents and parents, brothers and sisters, spouses and children—or at least some of these. And although her protagonists, for one reason or another, often leave home, "home"—and all that a definite place in the world implies—is a persistent concern of her fiction.[9] Her characters have a history, have attachments, and are products of their culture, though this is something they are not always ready or able to recognize. Her fiction does reflect a heightened sensitivity to the dangers of living. Yet it is a character's distance from "home," from a knowledge or an acceptance of his relation to the real world, that is often a measure of the dangers that await him.

In Oates's fiction, the individual is always viewed in the perspective of the larger world—most often, in the perspective of culture and history. Oates is an American writer self-consciously exploring the American experience. In a 1973 *Psychology Today* essay, she states: "All the books published under my name in the past 10 years have been formalized, complex propositions about the nature of personality and its relationship to a specific culture (contemporary America)."[10] Beneath her fiction's manifold and melodramatic surfaces, lies a vision of reality that may perhaps be best explored in the cultural context that Oates herself suggests and that her fiction and criticism confirm. This context is the pervasive idealism of American culture, the romance tradition of classic American literature, and the quintessentially American notion of freedom and self-sufficiency.

There is a peculiar uniformity to the most interesting of the descriptions that have been offered of the American imagination as it is reflected in our literature. The emphasis is on the individual negotiating the world in isolation and on the individual's refusal to accept the limits imposed by life in the world. D. H. Lawrence, for instance, portrayed classic American literature as "begotten by the self, in the self, the self made love." American writers wanted "Paradise," but writes Lawrence, "There is no paradise" (a phrase that Max, a character in Oates's *With Shuddering Fall*, echoes).[11] Mining these Lawrentian insights, Richard Poirier says of the protagonists in classic American literature: "They tend to substitute themselves for the world."[12]

And Ihab Hassan has perhaps grasped the underlying motive of American aspirations in his statement, "The anarchy of the American soul is nourished on an old dream: not freedom, not power, not
even love, but the dream of immortality. America
has never really acknowledged Time.[13]

In the American landscape evoked by these
descriptions, Joyce Carol Oates stands as a unique
and radical figure. She is a writer obsessed with
experiential plurality, with human reciprocity and
human limitation, and with reconciliation to time
and the manifest world. Oates is preoccupied with
the idea that the self is not a substitute for the world
but that a selfhood is possible only when it is located
in and delineated by a specific temporal and spatial
environment.

Characteristically, Oates's novels begin nearly
as paradigms of American history. As America
loosed its bonds from England, Oates's protagonists
find themselves by a variety of routes free from the
strictures of family, place, and history. Yet when
they attempt to follow the imperatives of the self,
they inevitably confront chaos, madness, or death.
In the romance tradition of American fiction, many
of Oates's characters strain to escape the world in
which they find themselves, but they are repeatedly
defeated. To survive, they are forced to acknowledge the world and respect its limits. *Wonderland*,
for instance, begins with Jesse Harte's escape from
his father's murderous gunfire. Orphaned because
his father has committed suicide after murdering his
family, Jesse undergoes a series of experiences,
each representing a period or aspect of American
history and culture, that cause him to withdraw further and further into himself, to depend solely on
the sufficiency of the self. In the end, however, he
comes to full, human consciousness by virtue of an

act of rescue and love. The overflow of the self to the world, implied by his act of rescue and love, is made a condition of his awakening from the solipsistic nightmare of his freedom.

In Oates, we are always made aware of our otherness. In her *Psychology Today* essay, "The Myth of the Isolated Artist," Oates writes, "In surrendering one's isolation, one does not surrender his own uniqueness; he only surrenders his isolation." In Oates's vision, freedom, in the sense of being above the restrictions of family, place, and society, is synonymous with isolation. She has made her artistic purposes very clear: "The novelist's obligation is to do no less than attempt the sanctification of the world!"[14]

Oates has D. H. Lawrence's suspicions about academic classifications of "high art." In an essay on Lawrence, she complains of R. P. Blackmur's judgment that Lawrence the "craftsman" did not often enough silence Lawrence the "demon of personal outburst." Her artistic alliance is, indeed, with writers like Lawrence rather than with more self-concious artists like James and Woolf. In a revealing analysis of these two writers she says, "But in the end we are somehow dissatisfied. We recognize the wonder of their aesthetic achievements, yet we must admit that the melodrama of Dostoyevsky and Stendhal has the power to move us more deeply." She disparages their "stubbornly monastic ... vision," asserting that "after James and Woolf, after the experiment of the mind's dissection of itself and its dissociation from the body, perhaps we are ready to *rediscover the world*" (emphasis mine). She argues against the strictures of New Criticism, which considers historical and cultural contexts as irrelevant to literary criticism, agreeing with Lawrence that "no poetry, not even the best, should be judged

as if it existed in the absolute . . . . Even the best
poetry . . . needs the penumbra of its own time and
place and circumstance to make it full and whole."[15]
With Oates's work, American fiction has abandoned
its raft, its forest, its whaling ship—what Poirier has
termed its "world elsewhere"—to reenter time and
history.[16]

Indeed in Oates's fiction, the sense of place
and history is essential. A reviewer has spoken of
her ability to "capture the spirit of a society at a
crucial point in history."[17] Yet despite her portraits
of man in society, her affinities with the American
Naturalists are minimal. Naturalism proposed that
"natural law and socio-economic influences are
more powerful than the human will."[18] It was preoccupied with social and biological inequity and la-
mented the downtrodden's impotence in the face
of materialistic, sociological, and biological forces.

Oates differs from the naturalists on philosophic grounds. It is not indignation against the
malevolent forces of heredity and environment that
vitalizes her art. Rather, heredity and environment
are simply the irrevocable conditions of our being
in the world. If we rise above the immediate circumstances of our birth, as Clara, the heroine of *A
Garden of Earthly Delights,* does, there is always
an external world which must be negotiated. Perhaps the most radical departure of her fiction from
that of the naturalists is in her depiction of the will.
In naturalistic fiction the human will is powerless
against external circumstances, while in Oates's fiction the destructive power of the will becomes one
of the author's primary targets.

Our romantic writers view the heroic stance, in
which the protagonist asserts his will against the
external world, as a liberating stance. For Oates this
stance is nihilistic, not heroic or liberating. In her

essay, "Melville and the Tragedy of Nihilism," Oates states that "the nightmare of *Moby Dick* . . . is not without redemption for us because we are made to understand continually that the quest, whether literal or metaphysical, *need not be taken* (emphasis mine). Later in the same essay, she argues that Melville dramatized "the plight of the Adamic man who loses his innocence and is precipitated to an immediate Faustian hubris and audacity."[19] These statements reveal Oates's inveterate antiromanticism, a position she continually clarifies in her criticism and repeatedly dramatizes in her fiction. She characterizes Sylvia Plath's poetry as the "death throes of romanticism," and in that same essay she asks, "Why does it never occur to romantic poets that they exist as much by right in the universe as any other creature . . .?"[20]

Oates views the obsessive drive for absolute freedom, for absolute control as symptomatic of narcissism or megalomania, as an instance of Faustian overreaching, which she regards as a tragic exercise in nihilism. To cite the example of *Expensive People*: matricide is the solution of the child-hero, Richard, to his mother's narcissistic assertion of freedom that denies him her love and recognition. Oates portrays suburbia, the setting of the novel, as an antithetical paradise into whose hallowed terrain one is admitted by virtue of one's greed. The dominant metaphor of the novel is, in fact, gluttony, which stands not only for excessive material acquisition, but more to the point, for an inflated sense of self that leads to a denial of the world, even as is the case with Richard's mother, Nada, a denial of one's children. Indeed, gluttony, obesity, and greed are the metaphors with which Oates repeatedly describes the excesses of will, the excesses of the isolated ego. In Oates, the efforts of the will are rewarded with a perverse form of liberation—with estrangement and alienation.

In *them*, based on the life story of one of her students, Oates describes the struggles of two poor urban adolescents to escape an environment that repeatedly erupts in violence. They attempt to live up to the American ideal of freedom, but inevitably, Jules and Maureen Wendall come up short against the unpredictable. Yet the unpredictable, in the form of beatings, murder, and race riots, is portrayed not so much as a result of sociological upheavals, as an insistent and pervasive rhythm of life. In a universe of caprice and chance, insists Oates, the individual who longs for freedom, for autonomy, is the most vulnerable. In the novel, the effort for freedom is slowly converted into an effort for association, connectedness, and roots. In the last scene of *them*, Maureen is married and pregnant, and her brother, Jules, hopes to find a job and get married. Marriage, pregnancy, jobs—the means by which the individual compromises his freedom and autonomy—are, in Oates, also the means by which the individual constructs barriers against a chaotic and threatening environment.

We can sympathize somewhat with reviewers who gloat over the violence in Oates. Her fiction does alarm and repel, but finally we must admit that what Oates does describe is an oppressive and insistent rhythm of American life. In answer to a question about the violence in her fiction, she said, "These things do not have to be contrived. This is America."[21] It is an America of race riots, migrant labor camps, suburban greed, motorcycle and race-car jocks, mail-order rifles, violent sex, volatile and hyperbolic adolescence, political assassination, family violence, self-proclaimed prophets preaching death and drugs—the America screaming from

the headlines of our daily presses. And Oates often
sets this "headline" picture of American life against
the larger canvas of American history. Her novels,
which often begin in the Thirties, give a sense of
the movement of American history. Behind the grip-
ping close-up of her characters' lives move the Great
Depression, World War II, the Civil Rights Movement, the Vietnam War, and John Kennedy's assassination.

Some writers have expressed a sense of defeat
when confronting the monster of American life.
Norman Mailer confesses that "The nature of existence cannot be felt any more. As novelists, we cannot locate our center of values."[22] Over two decades
ago, Philip Roth complained of the impossibility of
realistically portraying American life: "The American writer in the middle of the twentieth century
has his hands full in trying to understand, and then
make *credible* much of the American reality. It
stupefies, it sickens, it infuriates, and finally it is
even a kind of embarrassment to one's meager imagination. The actuality is continually outdoing our
talents and the culture tosses up figures almost daily
that are the envy of any novelist."[23]

Indeed as Raymond M. Olderman has noted,
many writers have met the challenge of current
American life by writing "fabulous" fictions. That
is, "Because experience tumbles fact and fiction,
fidelity to some concept of 'ordinary' experience
seems close to impossible. All ordinary experience
recedes into the fabulous ...."[24] Verisimilitude
yields to the broader, more exaggerated contours of
the fable. Along with the fabulators, Oates recognizes the fabulous quality in American life, but in
her writing she makes an extraordinary peace with
the reality of this life. Instead of writing fictions that
are more fabulous than the headlines, she uses these

headline events to form the plots of her stories. Her characters navigate through a world that is fabulous, but it is a world that is recognizably our own. Her characters are locked in history and time; they exist in and are vulnerable to American culture.

Although violence is a dominant mode of contemporary fiction, many contemporary writers, especially the fabulators, objectify the violent and absurd aspects of their culture. John Hawkes's *The Lime Twig*, for instance, competes with Oates's novels in the number and type of violent events it portrays, but it is a metaphorical violence, a projection of psychic images rather than of reality. Although these writers may not be conscious that they are subduing the beast of contemporary life by taking it out of real settings—indeed it is distinctly not the point for them—it is nevertheless an effect of their work. Oates, however, is usually meticulous in drawing her realistic settings so that when a fabulous event invades ordinary circumstances, it is jarring and disturbing because it is made part of the ordinary flow of time; it is not isolated by the imagination from life. It is less an aesthetic image projected by the imagination than it is an imitation, albeit melodramatic, of life. When in *Wonderland*, Monk, a psychotic guru-poet and ex-medical student, reveals to Jesse and his wife that he has stolen a uterus from a cadaver room, taken it home, broiled it, and eaten it, we are justifiably horrified. Our feeling stems from the fact that, given the circumstances, the event does not trespass the limits of possibility.

A typical example of Oates's manipulation of fabulous and realistic elements may be seen in her much anthologized story, "Where Are You Going, Where Have You Been."[25] Connie, the story's pretty, teenaged heroine, escapes her three year-old "ranch" house, her nagging mother who shuffles through the house in bedroom slippers, her older, staid sister, and the indifference of her father by going to a shopping mall several times a week where she joyfully passes the time in a teenage hang-out, sipping cokes, cruising for boys, enraptured by the omnipresent rock-and-roll music. The story develops in swift, realistic strokes until the Sunday that Connie stays home while her family goes to an aunt's barbecue. Connie sits in the sun dreaming of the boy she was with the night before, thinking "how nice he had been, how sweet it always was . . . sweet, gentle, the way it was in movies and promised in songs" When she opens her eyes, she is startled by the growing weeds and the "smallness" of her asbestos "ranch" house. This instance of shabby reality intruding on dream anticipates the incident with Arnold Friend on which the story centers. Arnold Friend drives up to her house unexpectedly and asks Connie to go for a ride. At first he seems the fulfillment of the teenage idol promised in the songs she listens to: everything about him seems strangely familiar to her—his open, gold jalopy, the faded jeans and boots covering his lean, muscular body, the expressions he uses. He seeks her out despite having seen her only once; he knows her name, her family, and details of her personal life. Rapidly, however, the fantasy deteriorates as we discover along with Connie that Arnold has the face of a thirty-year-old man; his boots are stuffed to make him appear taller; his talk is a rapid succession of echoes from songs of faded popularity; and his teasing, courting tone becomes insistent, threatening violence. What he "knows" about her, it is revealed, includes a psychic knowledge of what each member of the family is doing while he stands with Connie on her porch. She finally submits and goes with him. " 'My sweet little blue-eyed girl,' he said in a half sung sigh that had nothing to do with her brown eyes . . . ." Connie's "brown-eyed" individuality is submerged in someone's faded dream of the "blue-eyed" girl. And just as Arnold falls short of embodying a dream, it is suggested, so does Connie.

It is tempting to see Arnold as representing Mephistopheles, posing as "friend," seeming to fulfill dreams while only creating illusions, thus making the story simply a modern version of the struggle between man and the devil.[26] But if we resist this temptation, the story sounds a more authentic and original note. It is a story of an individual's betrayal by her dreams because reality makes of her dreams frightening hypocrisies. Connie is straining to transcend her "asbestos ranch house" existence. Her means of transcendence is adolescent culture. But just as America's straining toward its dream has brought a proliferation of asbestos ranch houses and shopping malls, adolescent culture has brought Connie thirty-year-old Arnold Friend. In each case the dream is the agent of betrayal because it proposes a freedom that is tragically impossible to realize in actuality. The paradox in much of Oates's fiction is that her characters push to transcend their circumstances, but it is their fate to discover that they are imprisoned in a dream polluted by the real circumstances of American life. Although the individual's dreams take the forms shaped by the ideals of his culture, the extent to which they are realizable is circumscribed by the realities of that culture.

Arnold represents life rather than the devil— friendly and ominous, glittering and tawdry, courting and malevolent, omniscient and ridiculous. He demands that Connie grow up, dispose of her banal dreams, and acknowledge and fulfill her sexuality.

He says, "I'm your lover. You don't know what that
is but you will . . . . I'll hold you so tight you won't
think you have to try to get away or pretend anything
because you'll know you can't." His hold is the hold
nature has over all life. Connie's fantasies must
yield to a more disturbing reality as dreams must
always yield to the realities of life. Where we are
going and where we have been is always the same
place, but the recognition of this fact is not easy to
make.

In "Where Are You Going, Where Have You
Been," Arnold Friend is created out of the stock
images of rock-and-roll songs, but his idealized
image is violated by limitations imposed by real
life—that dreams do not come true and that anyone
purporting to be a teenage idol should be checked
for a receding hairline.

Oates's insistence that society provides bound-
aries for existence and knowledge that cannot be
crossed, clearly distinguishes her fiction from much
classic and contemporary American fiction. According to Poirier, "What distinguishes" our fictional
heroes "is that there is nothing within the real
world, or in the systems which dominate it, that can
possibly satisfy their aspirations."[27] They create "a
world elsewhere," free from the mire of fact, where
the individual transcends the temporal and cultural
limits of his existence.

This need for transcendence, this dissatisfac-
tion with the American experience as a sustaining
and meaningful base for life, has often been traced
to the peculiarities of America's historical and political circumstances. As Tocqueville noted in *Democracy in America,* in a democracy "each citizen
is habitually engaged in the contemplation of a very
puny object: namely himself. If he ever looks

higher, he perceives only the immense form of a society at large, or the still more imposing aspect of mankind . . . . What lies between is a void."[28]

American fiction seems to acknowledge the truth of Tocqueville's observation. For the most part, our classic and contemporary writers have concentrated on the romance, with excursions into realism and naturalism, which the naturalist Frank Norris argued in "A Plea for Romantic Fiction" is also romance.[29] Much of our contemporary romance fiction is perhaps less a manifestation of twentieth-century experimentation than a symptom of America's history and political system. Because American writers have felt that there are no institutions which adequately mediate between the individual and the universe at large, the individual feels himself "dangling" between his puny life and the immensity of creation. The recourse has been to create "a world elsewhere."

This tendency of American fiction to ignore or subdue with fabulations the American experience has been encouraged by the facts of twentieth-century life—the holocaust; nuclear weapons; increased mobility; the faded power of family life, religion, ideology; and our "orgiastic" technological society.[30] However, Oates suggest that if these are the terms of our existence, then the escape into the "fabulous," into the isolation of our own fantasies and fears, is only an intensification of these terms, not a true liberation from them.[31]

In a critical essay on *Troilus and Cressida*, Oates reveals her concern with the limits that are imposed by life in the world. "Man is trapped within a temporal, physical world, and his rhetoric, his poetry, even his genius cannot free him. What is so modern about the play is its existential insistence upon the complete inability of man to transcend his fate." Later in the same essay she states, "There is a straining upward, an attempt on the part of the characters to truly transcend their predicaments. The predicaments, however, cannot be transcended because man is locked in the historical and the immediate."[32]

Thus Karen of *With Shuddering Fall*—after escaping the complacency and provinciality of her father's farm in order to chase the American dream of speed, danger, and big money, personified by the intense race-car driver Shar, and after enduring rape, violent beatings, a miscarriage, and the death of Shar—finds herself by the novel's end, back at her father's farm, even a little grateful to be a survivor. She tells herself, "When you are married—of course you will be married—deceive your husband each time you give yourself to him! But still you are alive and that is a miracle." There is a similar movement in *all* of Oates's novels: Elena, the heroine of *Do With Me What You Will*, spends most of the novel avoiding an engagement with the real by an almost psychotic passivity. At the end, however, she reenters time and history, earning her status as a survivor, by leaveing her husband, who sees her only as an object of beauty, and escaping with her lover, who wants her as a woman. In *The Assassins: A Book of Hours*, "only Stephen, who is willing to live an incomplete life, manages to survive."[33] The other main characters, Yvonne and Hugh, are destroyed by their inability to accept an "incomplete life," a life that will not yield to the mind's desire to understand, predict, and control.

In reply to a question about the themes in her fiction at a poetry reading, Oates stated that a recurring theme in her fiction is "recognizing limits."[34] Asked to enlarge on this statement, she explained, " 'Recognizing limits'—realizing that one cannot *know* the answers to mystery, and that one must nevertheless live with this predicament."[35] In Oates's fiction the dilemma of the imagination's limitless reach and the body's temporal and spatial restrictions is recurrently explored.

This dilemma is forcefully portrayed in the small masterpiece, "In the Region of Ice."[36] The protagonist, Sister Irene, who teaches literature at a small midwestern Catholic university, finds herself psychologically engaged with a frenetic Jewish student, Allen Weinstein, who believes that "ideas are real." He comes to dominate her literature class, and she thrives on the intellectual challenge of his questions although she is "terrified at what he was trying to do—he was trying to force her into a human relationship." When he fails to appear in class, Sister Irene feels injured. Some time later she receives a letter from him—he is in a mental institution—containing a disguised plea for help, threatening suicide. The nun accepts the mission, and in her excitement, feels "she understood now the secret, sweet wildness that Christ must have felt, giving himself for man, dying for the billions of men who would never know of him and never understand the sacrifice. For the first time she approached the realization of that great act." Yet there is a pathetic disparity between her feeling and her action. She manages to see Allen's parents and is bullied by his father to retreat. Months later, Allen pushes his way into her office, grasping for her hand, which she withdraws. He makes a desperate final plea for some sign of their communion, asking for enough money to escape to Canada. She refuses with "I can't help you, I'm sorry . . . ." He leaves her office hurling accusations: "I'm alive, I'm suffering—what does that mean? Does that mean nothing? I want something real and not this phony Christian love garbage—it's all in the books, it isn't personal—I want something real . . . ." When she later learns of his suicide, she muses, "She could only be one person in her lifetime. That was the ugly truth, she thought, that she could not really regret Weinstein's suffering and death; she had only one life and had already given it to someone else . . . ."

"In the Region of Ice" identifies, with deadly accuracy, the discrepancy between the beautiful ideals the individual's imagination proposes as his destiny and the pathetic reality of his fate. Sister Irene's image of herself as Christ-like is easily deflated by Mr. Weinstein's bullying. When confronted with Allen's demands and suffering, she retreats, icily submitting to the pressures of self-survival, preferring the anonymity of ordinary choices over the possibility of self-obliteration. To extend any part of herself to Allen—even a hand or some money—is to pass into another, unknown self. Only on the level of ideas—in her classroom—is she equal to his suffering and to a communion with him. The "region of ice" is the real which maintains its stubborn integrity despite the intense but transient fire of dreams. To violate it is to risk the loss of self, perhaps to sink with Allen into madness and death. Sister Irene is drawn to ordinary, not heroic proportions; her meanness is an exaggeration used to emphasize the theme rather than to indict ordinary choices.

Madness is the fate of the girl in "The Census Taker"—a denser and more complexly imagined story than "In the Region of Ice"—who is overpowered by the realization that the individual is helpless in asserting his will against the tide of time.[37] Mutability, transience, accident are the indomitable forces of nature that the census taker absurdly challenges in his attempt to document the

names and addresses of everyone living in Oriskany,
a remote community in Eden County.

The story begins in a fairy-tale cadence: "Some
time ago in Eden County, in the remote foothills of
Oriskany, the census taker of that area—a quiet
sleepy man in the thirty-eighth year of his life—
came one day to the last of the houses he was to
investigate." It is sunset and he looks at the tilted
mailbox on which is written "Robins" in "high, narrow, uncertain letters." The windows of the "forlorn" house look "blind," the land surrounding it
"distorted," and the sky "shrunken and artificial
and perverse." But he is relieved that for once the
map directing him is accurate. The map, the landscape, the house, even the mailbox mock his purpose, which is to fix, in the permanence of ink, a
community of lives. A member of the family, a girl
of twenty, "lifelessly thin," with large eyes hinting
at her visionary powers, asks him: "'a census begun
way two years back, ain't it? . . . Half them people
you got in that book are dead now or grown old or
different.' The census taker met her gaze with
shock. How could she have known his secret fear,
his secret horror? . . . . But he had consoled himself
with the thought that . . . once he had delivered the
book to the proper authorities, the reality that the
book suggested would become real, would have a
greater reality than any arbitrary juxtaposition of
human lives . . . . What did it matter that a man lived
or died, that he had four children or five, except as
it was recorded in the book?" This ironic rational-
ization summarizes the pathos of human efforts to
understand, to know, and to control, efforts that all
too often result in the creation of meaningless icons
to our inflated sense of power over nature.

As the story progresses, the boy and the girl of
the family tear down the layer of protective my-

thology in which the census taker has encased himself to block the ever-encroaching chaos of reality. The boy asks the census taker, "Ain't you afraid, goin' outside like that? With it gettin' so cold?" He relates the story of a man killed in a sudden snowstorm. The census taker counters, "But there are signs . . . . Ways of telling if a storm is coming—I have a list of them somewhere . . . . There is one about the clouds, if the clouds come over the northern mountains square . . . , then there's going to be a bad storm." The boy pierces this myth with, "The only way you do . . . is you look up an' its snowin' or somethin', or rainin', an' that's how you know."

As they wait for the return of the father, the only authority the census taker will accept to answer his official questions, the conversation becomes increasingly menacing. The girl reveals her madness, her intention through suicide to escape the impersonal hand of fate. When the census taker shows the family a picture of his house on the beach, the boy says, "Maybe it's all washed away, a tidal wave or somethin'." The girl adds, "or bomb." After a hysterical monologue delivered by the girl, the census taker, in the climactic scene, tells of his intention to leave. The mother asks, "But you ain't goin' to finish the census . . . . Why did you come?" The census taker replies, "Who am I to give you answers, to give you anything? Am I a man? Do I look like a man?"

The assumption underlying the census taker's question, "Am I a man?," is that a man can give answers; to be a man according to the census taker means to be able to solve the mysteries of life. Thus he denies his own humanity with his question, a denial prompted by his defeat in solving even the small mystery of the census. Of course, when the tension of the situation relaxes and the census taker

calms his hysteria by leaving the house, he is able
to blink the incident and restore his momentarily
lost mythology: "Looking toward the sky . . . he de-
cided—with deliberate, ruthless logic—that it was
really not going to storm that evening."

The story is brilliantly orchestrated. Each of the
four characters—the mother, the boy, the girl, the
census taker—are like musical notes vibrating with
increasing intensity and volume until all their com-
binations have been played and each of their relationships to the theme, which gathered them together, stands revealed. Three of the characters
refuse to acknowledge life's mysterious and unpredictable tides: the census taker finds protection in
his record book, his dream of his childhood beach
house, and his "storm" mythologies; the girl in her
madness; the mother in her kitchen, carefully avoiding questions that speak of things outside its walls.
Only the boy, with his limited vision and practical
intelligence, accepts the unpredictable nature of the
tides.

In Oates's fiction there is no alternative to facticity, to the multifold world. The individual's heroism depends not on the degree and kind of his rebellion but on the degree and kind of his initiation.
For Oates's American Adam there is no final reconciliation with God, no route back to Eden. Her
fiction documents the necessity for compromise,
reconciliation, association, and reciprocity. Reuel
Denney has said, "A student of American character
may say, as he usually does, that the American is
more American in his adolescence than at any other
time in his life."[38] In Oates's fiction, however, the
adolescent romance with freedom and immortality
has been discarded for the adult marriage to the
world.

2

~~~~~~~~~~~~~~~~~~~~~~~~~~~~~~~~~~~~~

The Ordeal of Initiation:
With Shuddering Fall

If freedom is the underlying theme of classic American fiction and its images of liberation are the raft, the ship, the forest, initiation is the underlying theme of Oates's fiction. In her fiction, freedom, not history, is the nightmare. Leslie Fiedler writes that underlying the American Gothic romances is "the fear that in destroying the old ego-ideals of church and state, the West has opened a way for the inruption of darkness: for insanity and the disintegration of the self."[1] In Oates's fiction this fear is hardened into reality; the "disintegration of the self" is the condition of freedom. For Oates, freedom is not the inaccessible condition, but almost a brutal fact of life in America. Characteristically, the initial events in her novels release her main characters from their paternal past, leaving them free, but also vulnerable to the assaults of darkness. Freedom becomes a greater burden than the lives they have left behind. Once the connections that have tied them to a particular identity in time are severed, they lose their foothold in life. The past they have left behind or were forced from is the past that holds their identity. To reclaim it, they must learn to suffer reality, resign themselves to its limitations, re-enter time and history, in order to live.

The pilgrimage towards freedom is reduced to

21

a process of initiation, "that critical encounter with experience the aim of which is confirmation into a social and moral order . . . . [It] entails reconciliation to time, endeavor in history, the final acceptance of death. In the process of initiation, dreams surrender to reality."[2] In Oates, as opposed to much American fiction in which the process of initiation "is either truncated or interminable," the process is completed by the character who proves himself a survivor.[3] Oates recurrently follows her survivors until they reclaim their place in time. The typical ending of an Oates novel images a character's return to "home" or places him within the context of marriage or in some other way restores him to the stream of history. He becomes a proof of the limitations of existence—that ordinary reality is the only reality that sustains life and that dreams are the province of the night.

In *With Shuddering Fall* (1964), Oates's first novel, initiation is a process of painful enlightenment, terminating in resignation and reconciliation. With this powerful and vivid first novel, Oates discovers and begins to define the territory in her fiction. The novel begins with idealized, romantic characters—a godlike, paternal figure, Herz; his virginal, religious daughter, Karen; and the violent rebel, Shar. In the broadest terms, the novel relates the story of Karen's initiation. This initiation is effected not by complete submission to an authoritarian order, represented by her father, but by a rejection of anarchy and chaos, represented by Shar. In this work, the encounter with chaos brings a recognition of the values of family, place, and history.

Oates portrays initiation as a condition which mediates between two types of anonymity: the anonymity that results from a complete surrender to a religious or social order and the anonymity that results from revolt, the defiance of the past which holds the inidividual's identity. Oates suggests that the American recoil against a life dominated by restrictive institutions has driven us too far in an opposite and just as dangerous direction, that we have substituted a self-isolating freedom for imprisoning conventions and traditions. Oates's position concurs with that of Frederic I. Carpenter who, in *American Literature and the Dream*, states, "American dreams erred, not in the direction of romantic absolutism, but of individualism."[4] *With Shuddering Fall* makes that final compromise between the isolation that is an imperative of freedom and the absorption that American idealism fears is an imperative of the community. It is a compromise which Fiedler asserts the American Gothic romances refused to make: "On the one hand, their fiction projects a fear of solitude which is the price of freedom; and on the other hand, an almost hysterical attack on all institutions which might inhibit that freedom or mitigate the solitude it breeds."[5]

Oates develops this theme of initiation through a reimagining of the biblical story of Abraham and Isaac. In an interview with Linda Kuehl, Oates said that "*With Shuddering Fall* was conceived as a religious work, where the father was the father of the Old Testament who gives a command to Abraham, and everything was parallel—very strictly parallel . . . ."[6] Indeed the parallel is evident: Herz is the fierce, Old Testament God who orders his faithful and devoted daughter Karen (Abraham) to kill Shar (Isaac), the only man she has found worthy of her love. Appropriately, Oates sets the Herz farm in a mountainous region called Eden County, thus emphasizing Herz's godlike role. Moreover, Herz has immense power. He has outlived four wives and his physical prowess is legendary. While Herz reads this biblical story to his family, when Karen is a child, she thinks, "What strange dignity to fulfill one's destiny in that way—forever bound by the inhuman plot of the story, manipulated by God Himself!" But this is Oates's portrait of Karen as a child; her attraction to this story of faith and obedience is the child's response to the order that nurtures and protects.

In her transformation of the biblical story, Oates diminishes the stature of Abraham's faith to that of the child's faith in its restricted, closed world before it breaks through to encounter the larger world. As God made Abraham his special child, Herz and Karen have a "special relationship." Yet Oates pictures it as a relationship that precludes growth and maturation. Karen, even at the age of seventeen, always feels eight or nine in her father's company. The imagery with which Oates describes her suggests she has not yet come alive, not yet made that crucial passage into experience. She is an ascetic child, with "pure white hair," susceptible to religious ecstasy. When we first see her, she is "queer" and "cold," and she has a "magic" control over her emotions. Even as a young girl she is able to create a "fog" that protects her from the painful taunts of overgrown, country school boys. She is prone to "try on" her father's grave site.

The novel's first book, entitled "Spring" relates Karen's ambiguous defiance of the dominating paternal order. The challenge to Herz's authority is anticipated by the unexpected arrival of Shar, a race-car driver associated with the tawdry glitter of the lowland towns, who returns to Eden County to visit his dying father, Rule. It is symbolized by Shar and Karen's accidental destruction of the bridge that leads to Herz's place, the bridge that Herz once promised the frightened child Karen would never break. The bridge represents Herz's power, the symbolic token of his authority and order. Its destruction, like the destruction of similar tokens of power in mythology, signifies his loss of authority and thus Karen's release from his domination. The bridge is also symbolic of Karen's maidenhead; thus its destruction foreshadows her loss of innocence and her final emergence from childhood.

The confrontation between Shar and Herz, which takes place at the scene of the accident, is the confrontation between an archaic order, based on obedience and faith, and a new order, based on defiance and self-assertion. Shar—his full name is Shar Rule, or "charred rule"—physically defeats Herz, deposing him from his seat of power. When we see Herz next, he has suffered a stroke. Unlike the God of Abraham, Herz is vulnerable.

Although Oates sees the necessity for the defeat of the old, religious order, she views the order which has replaced it, an order that Shar personifies, as just as deadly. Shar is a rebel figure whose triumph over Herz represents a triumph of anarchy and nihilism. In leaving Eden County, "It was not a life dominated by fathers Shar had fled, but a life of order, of meticulous heart-straining order." As a boy, "He had dreamed of lighting a gigantic torch and . . . burning all civilization . . . ."

It is in the soul of her heroine that Oates has the antithetical impulses, which Herz and Shar represent, do battle, and it is in Karen that these impulses are finally and brutally reconciled. Karen's motivations for her flight from Eden are deeply ambivalent. On the one hand, she, unlike Shar, does flee a "life dominated by fathers;" on the other hand, her flight from Eden to Shar follows on the heels of her father's commandment, which like God's to Abraham, is to kill the beloved, to kill Shar.

In her portrait of Karen, Oates associates freedom with anonymity. Karen's conscious motive in
following Shar to the lowland towns is to escape the
stifling provinciality of her birthplace, to capture the
freedom Shar seemed to represent. She seeks freedom, but freed from the past, she is also severed
from her identity which is rooted in that past. Once
she leaves her father, she is plagued by feelings of
anonymity: "All that made her herself, were confused, weakened, and she had nothing left to show
of herself but a face, a body, a set of emotions."
Unlike Shar, whose soul is his will, Karen's soul is
"defined only in terms of what it had surrendered
itself to: claims of blood and duty, to love, to religious ecstacy. In itself it had no existence . . . .
Karen realized she had no existence without the
greater presence of someone to acknowledge
her . . . ." It is this discovery about herself—that her
selfhood depends on an association with a larger
world—that finally prevents her from submitting to
Shar whose life is an attempt to refute this larger
world.

Shar embodies that aspect of the modern spirit
which Norman Mailer so well defines in "The
White Negro":

If the fate of twentieth-century man is to live with death
from adolescence to premature senescence, why then the
only life-accepting answer is to accept the terms of death,
to live with death as immediate danger, to divorce oneself
from society, to exist without roots, to set out on that un-
charted journey into the rebellious imperatives of the
self.[7]

Shar's energy and power, which make him a force
for freedom, are indeed linked to his power over
death. His freedom is based on a continual triumph-

ing over death on the race track; thus his freedom is also his prison. Oates, in a revision of Mailer, suggests that once the individual is separated from the web of associations that nurture his identity, he can feel his existence only in relation to death. In contrast to Mailer, Oates does not accept the deadly terms of this freedom, and her refusal is embodied in her heroine. When Shar finally offers Karen marriage, she declines because marriage to Shar would be a surrender to the nihilistic terms of his life. Karen does not submit to these severe conditions of his freedom, does not deny the claims of blood that such a submission would entail; she chooses initiation over the relinquishing of selfhood.

When Oates's protagonists risk anonymity for freedom, they often experience a sense of alienation from history. Following this pattern, Karen and Shar, after descending from their paternal home, feel suspended from the continuity of history. Karen "had withdrawn from history and had no interest in it, just as Shar . . . had no interest in it . . . ." This suspension of characters from a sense of history is a favorite Oatesian device. It suggests not their transcendence of time, as it would in romantic or religious works, but rather their rootlessness, their homelessness, their estrangement from the sustaining world.

Oates juxtaposes Herz's mountain with the lowland towns in which Shar makes his living. Yet this is not a juxtaposition of heaven and hell, though the towns are hellish, but a juxtaposition of two extreme orders, both incapable of nurturing human life without violating it. As the prevailing order of the mountain insists that the individual surrender his individuality, the prevailing order of the lowland towns insists that he is absolutely free. The one discourages self-assertion and emphasizes a suffocating conformity, while the other discourages association and community and promotes rebellion.

Oates vividly evokes these lowland towns that live by the quick money that the promise of violent thrills wrests from the transients and tourists who come attracted by the garish glory of race tracks, seedy bars, and neon lights. In her careful description of Cherry River, Oates depicts a town that has forgotton its history. In this depiction, she suggests that once history has been surrendered, anarchy and chaos take its place. For instance, when a "horde of boys" overturns and defaces a Civil War canon, nothing was done to repair the damage. The new people could not remember any such war and had no interest in it."

Like many American towns, Cherry River is a conglomeration of antagonistic groups of immigrants and races, pasted together by the commercial operations of "two or three gambling syndicates to the north." They shared little—not an ideology, or a religion, or historical roots—little but the town's name, and the summer visitors shared not even that.

Oates portrays Shar as the willing, yet ineffectual scapegoat for the spectators who watch him risk death to race around the track. In his last race, in which he commits suicide, Shar reflects that the spectators, who, in identifying with the drivers, "gave up their identities to risk violence," were "always cheated because the violence, when it came, could not touch them." Theirs is a "mock communion" because a scapegoat is the sacrifice of a community, and the spectators who watch Shar do not represent a community. They have come to Cherry River for its race track and its beaches, their lives dissociated from each other and from the town, and the speed and violence they witness together are an inadequate foundation for a sense of community. They have no common history; they are separate, and the sharing of death serves only to unleash rather than purge the violence within them. Thus Shar's sacrifice of himself, his suicide, becomes not an act of public expiation, but a private act of release from the anonymity of an isolated life, not joined to a community, a family, or by love to a woman.

The fact that a black driver, Vanilla Jones, wins the race is the excuse for the race riot that ensues. Finding an inadequate release in Shar's death, the people of Cherry River explode in an orgy of violence. They engage in a primitive communal baptism of blood that momentarily binds them together, giving them a shared experience that forms the basis for a temporary feeling of communion. Oates suggests that in a country that ignores even its short history, where a shared ideology, religion, and family life no longer serve as compelling bases for society, communal violence is a straining toward, a substitute for, a feeling of community and association.

In a critical essay, Oates writes that "nihilism is overcome by the breaking-down of the dikes between human beings, the flowing forth of passion . . . ."[8] That is, when the individual surrenders his isolation for an emotional association with others, he also surrenders nihilism. Oates dramatizes this belief in her portrait of Shar, whose nihilism yields to his passion for Karen. However, once Shar cedes his isolation for communion with Karen, he is doomed. When Karen rejects his love, he feels communion with the crowds who watch his suicide.[9] Shar's love for Karen redefines the terms of his existence, which comes to depend upon the communion of love rather than a triumph over death.

In a powerful and haunting image Oates creates an objective correlative for her sense of the disso- ciated life. At a freak show, Shar cannot watch the grotesque "contest" with the vulgar curiosity of his companions: "The contestants were without arms or legs, and lay on their sides, professionally, to show their faces. They were to race one another through sawdust to a red, white, and blue decorated finish line."

This is an image of life without love, of sheer will pulling the resisting hulks of bodies through time and space. For Shar it is an image of life with- out Karen. He regrets the day he found her because without her, without the vision of love, there would not exist for him the attendant vision of life's emp- tiness, of life without love. This recognition of the measure of his loss is the underlying motive for his suicide.

Oates's survivor, Karen, returns to the moun- tains, to her father, to her family in confused, bitter, and attenuated triumph. She has succeeded in being initiated, reaffirming the claims of blood, and es- tablishing her identity in the context of the things to which she is attached by blood. In Oates's world, maturity does not come through complete annihi- lation of the father and all that he represents, but rather through a discovery that the old paternal order, the order of time and history is the only bar- rier against darkness. Karen's initiation has been paid for with the loss of her lover, her baby (she has a miscarriage), and for a while her sanity (after Shar's death, she spends time in a mental institu- tion).

The terms of her initiation have been severe: just as Abraham was required to sacrifice Isaac, a return to her father required that she fulfill his com- mandment that Shar be sacrificed. However, in

Oates's revision of the biblical story, God (Herz) is not omnipotent, or Abraham (Karen) completely obedient, or Isaac (Shar) saved. Unlike Abraham's sacrifice that is a test of faith, Karen's sacrifice—executed by the witholding of her love—is a yielding of the "rebellious imperatives of the self" for a reentry into the larger world. Shar, as avatar of those imperatives, must die because in Oates's vision, as complete freedom implies a surrender of identity, identity implies a surrender of freedom. However, by demonstrating the vulnerability of this larger order—we recall Herz suffers a stroke—Karen has diminished its power so that when she returns, it is not in complete submission, but in reconciliation. Ihab Hassan, speaking of the heroines of Henry James, observes that "it is in sacrifice and not merely in refusal, that the complex imperatives of self and world are finally reconciled."[10] Karen has made that sacrifice and has achieved that reconciliation. Oates depicts her characters as straining upwards, yet all of their straining leads not to transcendence, but to a discovery of their relation to the finite world.

Since the main characters are inarticulate, uneducated, and emotion-driven, Oates puts the novel's philosophical statements in the mouth of Max, a greedy, overweight, and voyeuristic businessman whose neurotic obsession with his own health and safety forces him to live vicariously through the books he reads and the lives of the race-car drivers he manages. And although we cannot always trust his judgments, we can trust that the questions he raises are important. In speaking of John Milton's *Paradise Lost*, he says, "Temptation, sin, fall, and expiation, all around in a circle, into the garden and out of it, many angels, great blazes of rhetoric and light . . . . As if it mattered that there was ever a paradise, or

in what way it was lost to us—the only important
thing is that we have no paradise; we have none.
Yet a most beautiful poem! . . ."

Max expounds the tragic *Weltanschauung* that
underlies all of Joyce Carol Oates's fiction; that "we
have no paradise," but we do have "a most beautiful
poem"—that our imaginations have access to realms
denied to our bodies. In fact, two "paradises" have
been tested and rejected in this novel, Herz's authoritarian paradise, Eden, and the contemporary
paradise of freedom, represented by the lowland
towns.

Max is the first of Oates's megalomaniacs, those
devouring spirits who attempt to make life subservient to their will. Unlike Shar and Karen, who attempt a personal transcendence, Max and his counterparts in other of Oates's novels attempt, through
possession of things and people, to incorporate the
world in the self. Max's central myth is that "civilization" is a defense against chaos, against the primitive. He is a "bloated, insatiable spectator," finding
solace in the antiseptic world of the motel he owns,
which for him is an ultimate symbol of "civilization": "Now outside the sun would get in your eyes.
There would be mosquitoes or ticks or snakes—
bears, anything. A herd of cows with horns,
maybe . . . . But in here . . . there is no trouble—it
is all under control. This is what civilization brings
to us." This fancy is mocked by the ensuing race
riot that reduces his motel to rubble. The motel may
protect him against a "herd of cows with horns" but
not against the darker impulses of man. His error
is in imagining that his motel represents civilization, for a motel is, after all, an accommodation for
transients, emblematic of rootlessness, the antith-
esis of the Herz mountain home.

Max asks Karen, "and when your grave is lost,

where are you?" Karen's answer is the answer Oates characteristically gives, in one form or another, to all of her survivors, those who can accept paradise as only a poem. Karen says, "My grave will never be lost." She is determined that her life will not be lived in anonymity; that whatever happens to her, there are always the claims of blood; that her body has a place in the Herz graveyard. Although these claims represent her prison, they also represent her identity, and there her grave "will never be lost." In contrast, Shar, whose family ended with the death of his father, feels that "In such a vast world a man could never be himself for long, for a simple journey through time dissociated one identity from the other." But Karen's life is linked through the generations of Herzes to all of humanity, a humanity summed up by the puns the Herz name suggests: hurts, hearse, heart.

Oates contrasts Karen, whose identity as a Herz is her fate, with the Golyrod girl, who is offered to Shar as compensation of the loss of Karen and who is a "sinister, bloodless" parody of Karen. Her careful dress, her make up rituals, her sentences that begin inevitably with "I" delineate a personality whose identity is so tenuous, so dependent upon self-assertion, that it needs to be constantly put-on, maintained, exhibited. She is opposed to Karen who feels herself a void, whose identity is only real in the context of things larger than herself. The difference is that the larger context is permanent, while the identity of the Golyrod girl is transitory; it changes with her makeup and clothes. Karen's identity needs no cultivation—merely acceptance.

In the novel, Oates tells us that "Karen's sin and penance and expiation had . . . showed, probably in her eyes or somewhere in her face, the crushing justice of a moral universe." When asked to ex-

plain the possibility of a moral universe, Oates cited
the Stoics' philosophy that "Every man carries his
appointed fate with him."[11] Indeed, it seems that
in *With Shuddering Fall*, fate *is* a kind of morality.
As it is defined in the novel, fate, the circumstances
of one's personal history, imposes limitations without which human life would be a continuous encounter with darkness. Oates's is an American voice
urging a reconciliation between the individual and
his personal and collective history.

In an essay analyzing Sylvia Plath's cultural
significance, Oates refers to Plath's suicide as "the
fifth act of a tragedy, the first act of which began
centuries ago" when Renaissance man "wrenched"
the self from the suffocating grasp of God.[12] Oates
argues that the Renaissance assertion of the self has
led, by an inexorable process like that of tragedy,
to a severe intensification in modern times, so that,
as Plath exemplifies, the self is locked in its own
terrible isolation. *With Shuddering Fall* compresses
this same tragedy into two acts and adds a coda. In
Part I, "Spring," Karen, like Renaissance man, frees
herself from her godlike father. In Part II, "Summer," which takes place in the lowland towns, she,
like modern man, recognizes that the price of freedom is a loss of meaning, a feeling of anonymity.
But in Part III, "Fall," which we may consider a
coda that transforms the drama from tragedy into
comedy, Karen returns home to reclaim her selfhood. She does not succeed in defying her fate or
even rising above it; her redeeming act is to accept
that fate.

3

World Alienation:
A Garden of Earthly Delights

The idea of fate, the idea that one cannot transcend
the conditions of one's existence, is central to
Oates's vision. In *With Shuddering Fall*, it means
that Karen cannot escape the fact that she is a Herz;
to Oates man is an associated being, defined by the
circumstances of his life and by the circumstances
of his culture. She has said, "It's difficult for individuals to go beyond their culture, in terms of individuation, to break through to a higher, transpersonal set of ideals."[1] In her novels this "difficulty"
is repeatedly portrayed. Unlike romantic writers
who value the attempt of their protagonists to defy
or transcend their society, Oates sees meaning in
the defeat of this attempt because it demonstrates
what is for her a more compelling truth: that the
world cannot be defeated. Fate is thus an instrument of history, whether personal or collective, or
of culture, or of time; it is always an instrument of
those implacable forces that limit the horizons of
man's destiny. Oates's shift in the Romantics' emphasis on the heroic struggle to the inevitable defeat
may be gleaned from a passage in her essay on *Troilus and Cressida*. "Man's goals are fated to be less
than his ideals would have them and when he re-

alizes this truth he is 'enlightened' in the special
sense in which tragedy enlightens men—a flash of
bitter knowledge that immediately precedes death."[2]
For Oates enlightenment is a product of the defeat,
rather than a product of the struggle. Her aim is not
to sanctify the isolated hero, but, we remember, to
sanctify the world.[3]

Her next three novels—*A Garden of Earthly
Delights* (1967), *Expensive People* (1968), and *them*
(1969)—comprise a trilogy. These books, which
deal explicitly and self-consciously with American
culture, are set respectively in rural, suburban, and
urban America. According to Oates, they concern
"social and economic facts of life in America, com-
bined with unusually sensitive—but hopefully representative young men and women, who confront
the puzzle of American life in different ways and
come to different ends."[4] Despite the differences
among them in style and subject matter, each of
these novels describes the defeat of the romantic,
overreaching will that strives to overcome fate.

In Oates, the great symbol of American dislocation is the Depression. It is a palpable historical
symbol of dislocation because it is still within memory. If it has not immediately affected our lives, it
has affected the lives of our fathers. Indeed, Oates
has spoken of the impact the Depression had on her
father's life.[5] In *A Garden of Earthly Delights* and
Wonderland, and to a lesser extent in *them* and
Childwold, it is the initial impetus for the disintegration of an associated life, rooted to family and
place.

After the protagonists of *A Garden of Earthly
Delights* and *Wonderland* are deprived of their
pasts, of their family and home, by the Depression,
the crucial question for them becomes the creation
of a self that can be projected into the future. Dis-

located, they depend solely on the sufficiency of the self. In order to maintain that self, they begin to assert their will over their environment until the environment is subordinated to the isolated will, in a sense conquered by it.

The process by which the self becomes autonomous, by which the self is substituted for the world, repeatedly leads Oates's characters to a denial of their pasts. Oates often depicts this denial of the past through her characters' denial of the names with which they were born. Both Clara in *Garden of Earthly Delights* and Jesse in *Wonderland* disavow their surnames; this disavowal represents their refutation of their personal history and their attempt to create their own identity with nothing but their own volition. In fact, in a repudiation of her origins, Clara refuses to even remember her surname; and the underlying cause of her son's misery and his eventual suicide is this very repudiation of origins, which is a repudiation of his origins as well. Moreover, her son's Christian name is also changed— from Swan to Steven. In Oates, name is a metaphor for fate, and in attempting to change fate, which name changes imply, one risks an irrevocable alienation. The mother in *Expensive People*, for instance, changes her name from the prosaic "Nancy" to the exotic "Nada," but her new name betrays her accomplishment; she has exchanged "Nancy," signifying a person associated to the world in ordinary ways, for "Nada," signifying nothingness.

In *A Garden of Earthly Delights*, the dislocation that begins with the historical circumstance of the Depression is intensified by the assertion of the Faustian, overreaching will, which in conquering a world, begets megalomania, solipsism, and nihilism, stances of the homeless self. Unlike Karen (*With Shuddering Fall*), the protagonist does not find his way back home because he has no authentic "home" to which to return.

The book begins in the early 1920's and ends in the mid 1960's, and the great events that mark this period—the Depression, World War II, the postwar economic boom—serve not only to give the book a chronology that locates the action, but also to set the limits against which the individual strains.

The novel follows three generations of the Walpole family, from the land-and-family-oriented grandfather, Carleton, to the dispossessed and alienated grandson, Swan. The family's growth into dislocation is paralleled by the dislocation of the population of Tintern—where the novel's second and third sections are set—as well as America, by the Depression, war, and postwar industry. In Oates, the personal drama always reflects an historical or a cultural drama. Sons and fathers and husbands lose their share in the world during the Depression and have to work for others. Then they are torn from their families by war; everyone is set loose to encounter life on his own; the fine web of ties unknots, setting people adrift. And the increasing centralization of postwar industry and agriculture draws Tintern's population away until Tintern becomes a community of outsiders.

The novel's first section, "Carleton," opens with an accident on a country highway in Arkansas. A truck filled with migrant workers has collided with a car. The scene focuses on Carleton Walpole, whose wife, Pearl, gives birth to Clara, the central figure of the novel, in the back of the broken-down truck. In the background of the unfolding drama of the Walpoles lurk the misery and squalor of migrant laborers' lives and the barren landscapes of rural America. Carleton, who has lost his farm, is able to maintain his self-respect only because he sees migrant work as a means to saving enough money to reclaim his farm. Half of this section depicts Carleton's spiritual and physical deterioration as time makes of his farm a distant memory.

Oates portrays Carleton as a man whose self-hood, like Karen's, depends on a larger context. The metaphor Oates employs for this larger context is, significantly, "names." He can maintain a sense of self only by whispering "names" to himself: "names of his family first, then distant relatives, then neighbors, then distant neighbors . . . . Only when he felt that he had named everyone, and that he knew where he was among them, could he fall asleep." Events, however, break him down. With an "emotion like love" he kills his best friend, Rafe, in a barroom brawl; his wife dies in giving birth to her seventh child; another friend, Bert, is beaten by the local police for procuring for his own daughter; one of Carleton's daughters runs away ostensibly to get married; his son is scab-covered, strange, and bites off the heads of live birds to entertain his friends; and Clara, his favorite, runs off with a man she met in a bar. He dies of what seems to be intestinal cancer two months after Clara's disappearance.

However, Oates portrays Carleton's failure as only partially due to the intrusion of events that in nightmarish succession block his goal. The more compelling reason for his failure is the anachronistic nature of his goal. His father was a blacksmith; Carleton had grown up admiring families with eight children; he is land-oriented; he respects family structure, roots. He was forced from this life by an abstract power, by a national economic failure, his personal destiny controlled by agents he could not influence. He is locked in a time when migration is the condition of life.

The values that cause Carleton to associate his

identity with his lost farm and the family unit are
incongruous with a 1930's world where personal
destiny seems to be shaped to a great extent by national economic and political forces. The larger effect of these historical forces on the quality of
human life has been brilliantly defined by Hannah
Arendt. She describes the condition of the "loss of
a privately owned share in the world," the condition
of Carleton in the novel, as the first stage of "world
alienation."

"The first stage of this alienation was marked by its cruelty, the misery and material wretchedness it meant for
a steadily increasing number of 'laboring poor,' whom
expropriation deprived of the twofold protection of family
and property, that is, of a family-owned private share in
the world, which until the modern age had housed the
individual process and the laboring activity subject to its
necessities. The second stage was reached when society
became the subject of the new life process, as the family
had been its subject before. Membership in a social class
replaced the protection previously offered by membership in a family, and social solidarity became a very ef-
ficient substitute for the earlier, natural solidarity ruling
the family unit."[6]

Indeed Clara, as opposed to her father, aspires to
membership in a social class embodied by the
wealthy Revere, thus enacting the second stage of
world alienation as her father had enacted the first.
And although she never becomes truly accepted by
that social class, she is satisfied with the material
objects by which this class is identified.

Oates depicts Clara as an illiterate; therefore,
her consciousness is molded by what she sees and
experiences. As a child, she models her hopes for
the future, away from the migrant camps, on images
from school books—a white frame house, a smiling
family—from glossy magazine pictures of moun-

tains, castles, movie stars, and things, things, things; from a five-and-dime store whose goods represent all that she does not have and wants. In the book's second section, "Lowry," narrated mainly from the point of view of fifteen-year-old Clara, Lowry, the man with whom she escapes migrant life, establishes her in the town of Tintern. He finds her a job as a clerk in a five-and-dime store and a room to live in. Clara spends her time working and waiting for Lowry, idealizing him. To Clara, Lowry is different from her father and the other men she chances to meet whose "fathers had lost their land" and who "could not control anything."

At a friend's wedding, Clara meets Revere, who owns much of Tintern, employs most of its men, and whose second wife is a sickly, melancholy woman. Revere is attracted to Clara because she is "happy." When Lowry abandons the now pregnant Clara, fleeing to Mexico because of some illegal involvement, Clara, at sixteen, decides to take her "life into control." This decision marks her first important step in asserting the will as the primary instrument by which the self establishes an identity. In the second generation, Clara's, "home" is no longer a place to which to return. Rather, it becomes a place which must be won by almost Darwinian struggle. Clara gives herself over to Revere, who settles her on an unused farm, where she awaits the birth of her son, Swan, whom Revere believes to be his, and the death of Revere's wife.

Oates portrays the effects of the imperialistic will on the associated life through her portrait of Clara in the Revere household. Clara's introduction into the Revere household begins the process which finally results in the disintegration of the Revere family. Her manipulation directly and indirectly results in the death of one Revere son, the disinher-

itance of another, the disappearance of a third, and
the death of Revere himself. For Clara, the Revere
name signifies not a collection of related people
associated with a certain property, but merely a
wealthy social class. The intrusion of her materialistic values, and her appropriation of the name,
disrupts the family and leads to events that anni-
hilate it.

As Arendt's argument indicates, world alienation is a process through which the individual's relationship to existence becomes more and more abstract, until he feels completely alone, rootless and
purposeless. "Just as the family and its property
were replaced by class membership and national
territory, so mankind now begins to replace the na-
tionally bound societies, and the earth replaces the
limited state territory."[7] The process of world alienation, which began with Carleton, is completed
in the third generation by Clara's son, Swan. Swan
grows to adulthood in the hostile Revere household,
while Clara plots maniacally and successfully to
disinherit Revere's three sons so that her husband's
empire will fall, after his death, to her son. Clara's
purpose is to usurp a name and a world for her son
to inhabit, to establish his "fate" with her will.
While pregnant, Clara imagines her child "appear-
ing before the legs of aged people and pushing them
aside, impatiently, with somewhere to go . . . . It
would have a last name and a world and want nothing . . . ."

It is through the sheer power of will that Oates's
characters hope to overcome their dislocation, to
compel a sustaining world into existence.[8] And if
there is a failure underlying all of her protagonists'
struggles, it is the failure of will to compensate for
the loss of world, or in Swan's case, a loss of origins.
In Oates it is not history that lies at the heart of the

human tragedy—for history is irrevocable; one simply cannot contest it—but an extreme and finally
self-defeating assertion of will, self-defeating because it takes the individual even further into the
recesses of his isolation, even further from an authentic relation to his world. Despite all of Clara's
insistence and manipulation, Swan, even on the first
day of his arrival at the Revere house, feels out of
place. He voices his discomfort by noting that he
and his mother are encroaching on a world that is
clearly not theirs: "In the very air of this great stone
house there was an odor that could never have belonged to their own house—an odor of weight and
darkness and time . . . ."

For Oates, "fate" seems almost a mystical concept, representing our relationship to the whole
order of being. To violate this relationship is to violate the terms of our existence, to risk estrangement
from life itself. Curiously, Clara views Swan's success as dependent upon his rejection of his biological father, Lowry. After Lowry returns from war, he
offers to marry Clara, who is still waiting for Revere's wife's death, and to take her and Swan to
Canada. Clara refuses his offer because she wants
her son to have a "real" last name, a name that
wields power.

It is tempting to view the novel as simply a
moral allegory of American imperialism, of which
Clara is clearly an avatar. Yet with her portrait of
Swan, Oates is aiming at a more fundamental target.
She is attempting to show how will becomes an instrument of alienation. In the process of asserting
his will, the individual necessarily separates himself from the rest of being, and an extreme assertion
of will leads to estrangement from the rest of mankind. Thus, the imperialistic Clara begets a son
whose existential anxiety is rooted in the fact that

he does not know how he is related to the world; specifically, he does not know who his biological father is or his mother's maiden name. Oates portrays Swan as trapped between two identities, one biological and the other usurped. In this novel, ignorance of one's natural father, of one's origins, is a metaphor for world alienation. By refusing to tell Swan about his biological father, by telling him that she has forgotten her last name, and by insisting that he usurp the role of Revere's true sons, Clara creates the condition by which dislocation, the legacy of history, is intensified to a complete dissociation from the world.

In creating Swan, Oates may have had in mind James Joyce's hero, Stephen Dedalus, who throughout *Ulysses* is on a journey to his spiritual father, Bloom.[9] Indeed, when Swan enters the Revere household, his name, we remember, is changed to Steven. Moreover, "Swan," that majestic bird, may have been suggested by "Dedalus," the mythic artist who wanted to give man wings. Stephen Dedalus, like Swan, is preoccupied with the idea of fatherhood. He says,

Fatherhood, in the sense of conscious begetting, is unknown to man. It is a mystical estate, an apostolic succession, from only begetter to only begotten. On that mystery . . . the church is founded and founded irremovably because founded, like the world, macro- and micro-cosm, upon the void.[10]

One implication of Stephen's theory, which is at bottom a theory of knowledge, is that the yearning for God, the Father, is a yearning to uncover the mystery of one's source; it is a yearning never to be fulfilled because fatherhood as a "mystical estate," one can never *know,* absolutely and finally, who one's father is.

For Stephens Dedalus, the profound sense of insecurity and alienation that results from the mystery of one's source is the basis of religion which promises to lead the individual back to the source of all life, back to God, the Father. Oates, however, places a different emphasis on the notion of fatherhood, of sources. She is concerned with the ways by which the individual isolates himself or is isolated from the world. Thus an acceptance of the father is an acceptance of otherness. It implies that the individual is not alone, but is fundamentally, existentially connected and related to the world. It is this connection and this relation that for Oates defines his identity.

Oates's novels are populated with characters who believe themselves self-created, who often declare themselves their own progenitors. For Oates this declaration is not a symptom of their autonomy, but of their alienation. In audaciously denying their fathers, they deny the source of their being and thus assert merely their homelessness. To Swan, like Dedalus, fatherhood is a mystery. However, this is not a condition *he* has willed, but a condition bequeathed to him by his mother. Swan ponders the meaning of having a father: He "could not quite understand what it meant to have a father," and at the "very heart" of the relationship between Revere and himself, he feels a "forlorn emptiness." Swan has no model for self-definition, none even that he can defy or reject. Moreover, hovering above him and struggling within him is an inchoate recognition of his biological father, who is, "vague and remote but somehow more vivid than Revere." Clara characterizes the relationship between Swan and Lowry:

"The relationships between people and their fathers were like thin, nearly invisible wires . . . you might forget they were there but you never got rid of them."

Oates portrays Swan's struggle for identity as a struggle between his will and an essential self that refuses to be transformed. A secret discovery of his mother's name, Walpole, leaves him trembling; against this name "he said his real name out loud so that he wouldn't forget it: it was Steven Revere." His "world alienation" is continually reiterated in the third section of the novel, entitled "Swan." In a study hall "he felt as if he were an alien in this room, waiting patiently for the time to come when he could return to his proper place."

Karen returns to Eden County to reclaim her identity, but Swan has no such place. He has no grasp of his past so that he can project himself into a future. His life has been willed into existence, manufactured like an artifact by Clara; he was born the son of an usurper, a son who cannot accept his parent's deed. In a revealing passage, Swan acknowledges that his appropriation of the Revere name violates all that this name represents: "He liked to think that he was dragging them all up with him, all those legendary Reveres, those dead old men and women who had loved and hated one another so fiercely, bound together by a single name and committed forever to living out the drama of that name."

Some reviewers have complained of the "Swan" section in the novel. Richard Clark Sterne says, "The last third of [the novel], dealing chiefly with 'Swan' and Revere, seems diffuse, less carefully worked out than the superbly controlled first part about Carleton, or the complex, vivid second part which focuses on Clara."[11] Page Stegner asserts that "when the focus wings away from Clara and onto Swan, the novel seems to lose some of its drive . . . . As a character he is less interesting than the others, and as a result his portion of the novel . . . is . . . a letdown."[12] What these reviewers have failed to see is that the book's narrative drive is toward Swan because it is in him that the modern condition, the result of the progressive abstraction of our relation to existence is mirrored.

Indeed, each male character whom Clara encounters has a progressively more abstract idea of what causes his unhappiness. For Carleton it is the loss of his privately owned share in the world—his farm. For Lowry it is his vision of life—"Everything's bleeding to death. I can see it."—that causes him to search for a healing "voice." For Revere happiness is represented by the childhood memory of a blonde immigrant girl whose image he tries to recapture by marrying Clara. Each wants to recapture an Eden, to release himself from the unhappy burden of experience. With Swan, however, Eden can no longer even be articulated; the ideal can no longer be imagined.

In this novel, as the individual's relation to existence becomes more and more abstract, as existence grows further from a dependence on place and family, the individual responds by withdrawing his libido from the outside world. The libido becomes introverted, attached to the self. This condition results in solipsism, personified by the final Carleton and the initial Lowry; nihilism, personified by the final Swan; and megalomania, personified by Clara. These are, to reiterate, the stances of the homeless self, of the self that is deprived of a real and authentic relation to the world. In the land and family-oriented Carleton, libido is still attached to the outside world. He "had a terror of things getting

lost . . . . If anything got lost it would be that much
harder to get home again . . . ."

Oates images Carleton's straining to control his
life against an amorphous mass of forces and events
in his vision of a highway: "He saw a picture of a
barren highway, empty highway stretching off into
the distance, and on either side of the highway vegetation he had never bothered to look at, an entan-
glement of bushes and trees and weeds writhing in
their own silence, tensing steadily against whatever
held them back or whatever kept them from rushing
upon the road and overwhelming it." Against this
threat, he asserts his name, his identity, and his
memories, but in a curious and telling way: "Everything—everyone—the whole world—was joined in
him. Only in Carleton Walpole. He was the center
of the world, the universe, and without him everything would fall into pieces." This statement is a
bald assertion of solipsism; the process whereby the
individual substitutes himself for the world, whereby
the libido becomes introverted, has begun. When
the world is lost, the self is all that remains as a
barrier against the void. Thus Oates's characters, in
rebuilding the world, attempt to house it in the self.

Yet the true solipsist of the novel is Lowry, who,
curiously, physically resembles Carleton and whose
parents were also migrants. Clara models herself on
Lowry whom she believes has the control her father
and his kind never had. Yet Lowry's "control" is a
function of his solipsistic existence, a result of his
denying his ties to the world. When Clara confesses
a helpless love for her family, Lowry says, "I was
born to help such things . . . . I'd like to have everything I owned in one bag and take it with me . . . .
Once you own things you have to be afraid of them.
Of losing them." His control, though, is a negative

attribute, maintained by denying his past and by denying his ties to the world.

Carleton's failure is his failure to recapture a sense of place, a source for his existence, with which he identified his selfhood. Lowry has internalized this sense of place, has substituted solipsism for life rooted in the world, and like the final Carleton, has housed the world in the self. He feels that his identity needs nothing to anchor it, but his claim that he is a world unto himself is belied by his "insatiable yearning" for a "voice."

Oates portrays the eclipsing of Lowry's solipsism as resulting from his participation in two archetypal situations of man in society—marriage and war. The woman he marries in Mexico, whom he thought embodied the longed for "voice," turns into a prosaic, nagging wife. Still searching for this "voice," he enlists in the Army and is sent to Europe, where he turns thirty and is wounded. He cannot withstand the experience of war, where his solipsism melts in the heat of battle, and he becomes vulnerable to his common humanity. In Oates, the confrontation with facticity often signals the subduing of the presuming will. His antidote to his European experience is to marry Clara and take their son to Canada, where he intends to buy a farm. Like Carleton, he now wants a life associated with place and family; he wants a context for his own identity. Lowry's character development is a reverse of Carleton's. As Carleton begins with the wish to recapture a share of the land and ends as a solipsist, Lowry begins as a solipsist and ends by longing for a share in the land.

In *A Garden of Earthly Delights*, the individual's relationship to the land, like his relationship to fathers and to his name, defines his relationship

to the world. For the world-alienated Swan, the land
is no longer a context for his identity but a context
for his anonymity, a place in which to hide from the
struggle for identity: "This vast sweep of land and
sky was something that could hide you. Even the
dead white of winter could hide you, flaking gently
over you, and nobody would need to put a tomb-
stone up to keep your name remembered because
there would be no name to be remembered . . . ."

In fact, Oates juxtaposes two ideas of landscape,
the one ideal and the other nightmarish. The main
action of the novel takes place in Tintern, which
before the war "was settled deep into the ground."
The town's name suggests Wordsworth's "Lines
Written a Few Miles Above Tintern Abbey." The
poem recaptures a nostalgic moment in which the
poet feels his "eye made quiet by the power" of
nature's "harmony," a moment in which he can escape "the heavy and weary weight/Of all this un-
intelligible world."[13] It is this "weight" that Carleton and the final Lowry wish to escape and this
"harmony" they long to capture with their share in
the land. But between the ideal and the real has
fallen the shadow of history.

With Swan, Oates's world-alienated man, the
relation to being is so abstract, the ideal is so blurred
by his ambivalence, that it finally dissipates, leaving
only the contorted landscape of Bosch's "The Garden of Earthly Delights" after which the novel is
named.[14] The three panels of Bosch's triptych de-
pict "respectively, the creation of Eve in Eden, the
debauchery of her descendants in the earthly garden of delights, and the punishment of mankind in
hell."[15] Bosch's nightmarish panels in which grotesque, gigantic birds and vegetation dominate, in-
form much of the imagery of Swan's section in the
book.[16] In fact, the title of the book, according to

Oates, is "Swan's title for the story of his life."[17] Swan, who feels his identity has been usurped, projects a predatory image of existence. Lowry's presence is felt by Swan as a "bird circling slowly to the earth, its wings outstretched in a lazy threat."

In the episode that ends with the death of Robert, Swan's stepbrother, whom he has accidentally shot while hunting, Swan imagines the woods filled with predatory birds—"killers"—chicken hawks, grackles, crows, mocking his own reluctance to be a predator. He feels he can win Revere's love only by becoming a predator himself, by "draining the blood of birds and animals." He envisions the spirit of God as a bird of prey, like a chicken hawk. Moreover, he recognizes that there is a predator within him struggling to get out, threatening to overcome his life. He acknowledges that "he was a killer who had not finished with his work yet but was waiting for his deed to rise up in him . . . ."

It is this predatory landscape, Oates is suggesting, that is the legacy of the imperialistic will, Clara's legacy. When the establishment of self depends solely on the assertion of will, success is determined by one's predatory powers, by one's ability to be victorious in a Darwinian struggle. It is ironic that Clara, who is responsible for shaping the world into Boschean proportions for Swan, is the only character who even momentarily finds Wordsworthian harmony: she finds it in her garden, which she cultivates while waiting for Revere's wife to die. "The garden was as much of the world as she wanted because it was all that she could handle . . . ." In her garden, "she would stand transfixed, as if she were at the threshold of a magic world." It is ironic, too, that Lowry offers her this kind of world and that she rejects it.

For Clara, who, as suggested, is an embodiment

of American imperialism, Wordsworthian harmony with nature is no longer a compelling idea. The hope for conquest, not harmony motivates her actions. Faust, not Wordsworth, is her true romantic ancestor; and it is finally Faust's legacy, Oates suggests, with which we must grapple.

The value of Clara's assertion of will is judged in the end by its results. In the climactic scene, Swan, now a young man whose violent ambivalence toward the Revere name and wealth builds to an intolerable level, confronts Clara and Revere with a gun. His intention is to kill Clara, but when she calls him "weak," because he does not have the strength of will to assume his usurped role, he shoots Revere and himself, resolving his ambivalence in nihilism.

In Oates's vision, the world that the will forces into existence is a world that leaves behind no legacy and which is finally not self-serving. Indeed, Oates ends the novel with an ironic image of Clara in middle age: She is subject to moments of paralysis; the entire Revere fortune is used to support her existence in a nursing home, where she spends her time watching television programs "that showed men fighting . . . killing the enemy again and again until the dying gasps of evil men were only a certain familiar rhythm away from the opening blasts of commercials, which changed only gradually over the years." In these television shows, she watches versions of the Darwinian drama of her life. Clara's megalomania has finally defeated her. The "home" she has won is a place where senescent, homeless strangers await death. Ironically, her efforts have succeeded in providing her with only enough money to sustain her homelessness in style.

Finally, however, we do not feel moral outrage at Clara's actions; we merely observe her and even admire, just a little, her audacity, her success. And though we admit that she deserves her end, we also admit that Swan does not. He is a type of modern man, struggling against his own dislocation and incoherence, his "world alienation," inheriting a conflict he cannot satisfactorily resolve. We sympathize with his view of existence as a grotesque Boschean landscape. Although the assumption which vitalizes the art of the religious painter Bosch—that life is a struggle between good and evil—is not Oates's, or ours, the image of existence that he creates is perhaps a valid representation of the fruits of a greedy and imperialistic assertion of will that not only intensifies the individual's isolation, but that makes of him a predator who stalks the world, and stalks it alone.

4

The Gluttons Dream America:
Expensive People

Expensive People (1968) is an extravagant experiment, radically different in style and development from Joyce Carol Oates's previous books and idiosyncratic even in the light of her later works, although the deeper concerns of this novel reflect the general preoccupations of her works. It is the story of eleven-year-old Richard Everett, who kills his mother, Nada. One reviewer sees Richard as an "11-year-old Joe Christmas in bifocals and blue blazer, blasting away at his mother," and Richard himself asks the reader to imagine him as "Hamlet stunted at eleven years of age."[1] The book is in that American novelistic tradition of family violence in which one family member murders another, oppressing family member.[2] Fiedler in *Love and Death in the American Novel* suggests that much of the best of American fiction is a parable of the rebellious child, America, engaged in an ambivalent effort to wrest itself from the domination of mother England.[3] Perhaps working in this tradition, Norman Mailer has made uxoricide—from mother to wife is a small leap in a post-Freudian era—a condition of the American Dream, and the fictional mothers in *Portnoy's Complaint* (published in 1969, a year after *Expensive*

People), and *A Mother's Kisses* make matricide seem
not only justifiable, but a heroic ideal. In these
cases, the victims of domination want to be free to
travel the road of self-actualization, unfettered by
both the fatuous or outmoded values of their oppressors and the love or guilt that keeps these victims enthralled. In the mode of American romanticism, the goal is autonomy.

In *Expensive People*, however, this tradition is
subjected to a characteristic Oatesian twist. Here
the goal is not autonomy but reciprocity, relationship, connectedness. Richard *yearns* for a mother
like that of Portnoy. The mother, Nada, like her fictional counterparts, imposes impossible goals on
her son, but unlike these counterparts, her underlying purpose is not his complete dependence and
submission. Rather, she wants him to be totally free
so that she, in turn, can be totally free of him. Con-
versely, Richard does not want freedom from Nada.
Indeed, his greatest fear is that she will abandon
him. Richard presents another approach to the problem of initiation: Karen Herz survives the process
of initiation by reaching a compromise between father, self, and world; Swan Revere can find no authentic context for his identity in order for the process of initiation to take place; but Richard, by killing
his mother, arrests the process before it severs his
dependence on his mother and joins him to a world
that is portrayed as graceless and jaded, where people pursue not one another—which would at least
signify an acknowledgement of their relatedness—
but merely their own peculiar hallucinations. The
story offers a variation of the Freudian romance.
Instead of killing his father in order to marry his
mother, Richard kills his mother in order to establish an irrevocable relationship between them, that
of killer and victim. In Oates's suburban paradise,

human associations are so elusive, so slippery—
even those between mother and son—that only
murder guarantees their stability.

As Oates employs the metaphor of fatherhood
in *A Garden of Earthly Delights*, she here employs
the metaphor of motherhood. In *Expensive People*,
it is not the mothers who vigilantly guard their children, but the children who must vigilantly guard
their mothers because they are in constant danger
of falling into madness or more to the point, aban-
doning their children. Richard employs laundry
chutes, stairwells, telephone extensions, and many
modes of dissembling in order to spy on his mother.
Gustave, Richard's friend, in a characteristic un-
derstatement, points out to him, "You should understand that it's always an awkward situation. Having a mother, I mean." And Richard, in a characteristic
overstatement, which nevertheless contains some
truth, asserts, "They're all trying to kill us, it's nothing personal." By portraying the nurturing relationship between mother and child as fragile and vulnerable, Oates reverses the assumptions of our
romantic writers who, according to Fiedler, are intent on escaping the domination of parents or of
mother England. The novel parodies American romances by inverting the quest for freedom into a
quest for bondage, for in Oates's scheme freedom
is not synonymous with self-fulfillment but, as we
have seen, with alienation.

As have many of Oates's novels, this novel has
a triptych structure. In the first part, Richard confesses his matricide; the family moves to Fernwood;
Nada abandons son and husband for the third time;
and Father tells Richard that Nada had wanted an
abortion when she was pregnant with him. Part One
ends with Richard's destruction of the Records'
Room of the Johns Behemoth Boys' School. In Part

Two, Richard secretly reads the notebook in which
Nada, who is a writer, scribbles her ideas for stories;
they move to an even more expensive house in
Cedar Grove, where Nada reappears; Richard reads
Nada's story, "The Molester," and thereupon pur-
chases a mail-order rifle. In Part Three, Nada again
betrays Richard and his father with a lover; Richard
attends a lecture on sexuality; he has a mad spell
in a flower bed; he hides in a closet and overhears
Nada and her lover; he begins his career as a sniper,
going out three times, purposely missing the victims, and the fourth time he kills Nada. He discovers
that Nada was born Nancy Romanow, daughter of
poor immigrants; he sees psychiatrists, and his father remarries. At eighteen he writes his memoir in
a one-room apartment and eats his way into obesity.

The novel is polyphonic, mixing elements of
black humor, surrealism, the grotesque, social realism, and especially parody within the psychologically realistic framework of Richard's confession.
It is interspersed with lectures on writing memoirs
and the nature of fiction and is documented with
references to historical child criminals and gluttons.
It even contains some imaginary reviews of the
novel in prestigious journals. By employing all of
this machinery, Oates creates the sense of a memoir
that might have been written by a very unhappy,
fat, neurotic, overly sensitive, brilliant eighteen-
year-old who killed his mother at the age of eleven
and got away with it.

The world of *Expensive People* is a Salinger
world, enlarged, caricatured, and edged with per-
versity.[4] Of Salinger, Fiedler writes: "not junkies
or faggots, or even upper bohemians, his chief characters travel a road which leads from home to school
and from school either back home again or to the
nut house, or both. They have families and teachers

and psychiatrists rather than lovers or friends."[5] These elements are also present in *Expensive People*, but they are enlarged to almost gargantuan proportions, betraying the dual hysteria of the narrator and the world about which he writes. Home in this novel is an English Tudor, "a bastardized French-American affair," a baronial Georgian, or a fake Scandanavian set primly on Burning Bush Way or Labyrinth Drive in communties called Arcadia Pass or Pleasure Dells or Bornwell Pass.

We are thrust into a world where the commonplace becomes a source of menace. Richard attends an Anglophile school called Johns *Behemoth* Boys' School. Richard describes the Humanities Building as having a "surly, encrusted look, its windows like multiple eyes with thick, leafless vines over them like eyebrows." Indeed, the entrance exams for ten-year-old boys contain questions with "multiple eyes" for these precocious but defenseless victims, such as: "If you came upon two cows mating, which would you do? (1) Hide your eyes (2) Take a picture (3) Call your friends to look (4) Chase the cows away."

Oates uses suburbia to satirize and parody various aspects of the romantic imagination. Primarily, suburbia and suburbanites represent the consequences of romantic overreaching. Not only does Oates satirize the romantic quest for freedom in her portrayal of Nada and Richard, but she satirizes the quest for adventure, for exotic experiences, and the quest for a paradise on earth. As freedom is equated with narcissistic cruelty, exemplified by Nada, adventure is equated with aimlessness, and paradise is equated, in a curious and ironic way, with stagnation. All of these quests are the quests of the adults in the novel, and by juxtaposing them to the simpler and more urgent quests of the children,

Oates deepens the satire until it borders in some respects on tragedy.

Oates suggests that romantic dreams are a form of spiritual gluttony that feed man's sense of self-importance but in the end betray him by estranging him from all that is truly vital in life. In fact, as landscapes become the metaphors for individual lives in the rural tale, *A Garden of Earthly Delights,* so gluttony, the deadly sin, and vomit, its consequence, become the pervasive symbols in this tale of affluent suburbia, and perhaps because his hunger and his need for protective layers of fat is the greatest, Richard becomes the most voracious glutton in it. Richard vomits at his entrance exams to Johns Behemoth and again when he destroys the Records' Room. He gorges himself until his body swells to 250 pounds after Nada's death, while writing the memoir. Richard prepares us for the motif of gluttony when he relates the tale of Nada's uncle, who "committed suicide by overeating." until the lining of his stomach burst. He documents this motif with the stories of Juvenal, who ate "until he was sick, out of pure spite at the heaven of sensuality he could not enter," and Laurence Sterne and Charles Churchill, who "came to London (but not together), lunatic, depraved gluttons of clergymen whose only aim in life was to devour as much of anything as was available!—and all of history gives us these weird writers . . . coming to London or Rome or New York, anywhere, to fill their stomachs and brains with whatever was handy."He compares these to Nada: "But even as Juvenal vomited as he ate, so Nada did vomit back out much of what she took in so eagerly; and even as Sterne and Churchill met their ends in excess, so did Nada invite her finish by an excess of greed."

Gluttony is not only a metaphor for suburbia in

Expensive People, but it is also a metaphor for all
of those individuals who aspire to transcend their
limitations. It is a gluttony that here stands for the
Faustian overreaching, the Quixotean madness,
from which all of humanity suffers, to get beyond
itself, to ascend into its own "hallucinations." In
this novel, it is gluttony that produces suburban
paradise, gluttony that motivates Nada's abandon-
ments and her refusal to accept responsibility for
her son, gluttony that prompts the aimless adventures of these expensive people, and gluttony that
goads Richard into committing matricide. Humanity's greed for paradise on earth, for freedom, or for
the ideal is never satisfied, though overpresent, and
it is this archetypal conflict between aspiration and
limitation that is one source of energy for Oates's
novels.

Gluttony is thus a negative symbol of romanticism, and it is romanticism in its various guises
that is Oates's target. Much of the comedy in the
novel comes from Oates's satiric portrait of suburban fathers as modern versions of Arthurian heroes.
These modern knight-errants ride Lincolns and jets
instead of chargers; they work for companies called
GKS, OOP, BOX, or BWK that make, for instance,
mysterious wires for detonators in bombs in order
to win their one-hundred-thousand-dollar houses.
Their adventures are purposeless, schizophrenic—
they have a certain form and inner logic, but are
indiscriminate, without discernable rational motivation. They are knights who do not know for what
ideals they are fighting or who the enemy is. For
instance, Oates offers a satiric catalogue of the activities of Mr. Hofstadter, Richard's friend's father,
who "was in oil and rarely seen." His enterprises
include dining with princes, riding jeeps in the
Near East, sleeping with vermin "just for fun," mak-

ing a religious pilgrimage to Jerusalem, surfing in California, having an audience with the Pope; Oates ends the catalogue with his listening to Baxterhouse's "Symphony for Silence."

Oates underscores the frenetic aimlessness of Mr. Hofstadter's adventures by placing them in an appropriately ironic framework: In the first sentence he is "rarely seen," and in the last sentence, he is listening to a "Symphony for Silence," signifying the value of the activity in between. The male suburbanite, Oates style, is the man of the gratuitous gesture, for whom appearance substitutes for reality and for whom form replaces belief and commitment. The passage seems close to the extravagances of Pynchon or Barthelme, or, to cite the older tradition, the picaresque. Yet the comedy is submerged in a note of pathos, for these adventures are related by the children from whose desperate viewpoint Oates never allows us to divorce ourselves.

Oates's characters, in an imitation of heroism, are continually searching for enemies to overcome. However, because their true enemies are unknown to them, these expensive people battle faulty garage doors, cars in parking lots, freeway traffic, or chipmunks that have invaded the basement. In one episode, Oates parodies a battle scene in her description of Mr. Hofstadter driving on the expressway: "As the 'driving' set upon him . . . his neck [grew] thicker and stronger as if preparing for battle . . . . His hands gripped the wheel the way they might have gripped any weapon, with confidence and pride and barely restrained vengeance."

Hofstadter and his counterparts are highly competitive, natural warriors without a war, a cause, or a visible enemy. Yet the perception underlying all of these absurd battles is that the enemy is not outside but inside. It is an enemy who urges us to expend our energy in the name of some "transpersonal ideal," to which, in Oates's outrageous parody of romantic aspirations, entry is thought to be gained by doing battle on a freeway.

Oates portrays suburbia as a perverse burlesque of Western Civilization where aspects of our history and culture are devalued, turned into place and people names. El Dorado is a beauty parlor; Medusa is a hair style; Behemoth a boys school; Labyrinth, Bunker Hill, Arcadia, Burning Bush are street names; ancient Egypt is preserved in dangling jewelry; Dante an excuse for a women's club meeting, Pandora a socialite, Voyd a lawyer. Its love goddesses are parodies of Venus. Pictured in *Vogue* is the Duchessa of *Vile*sia [emphasis mine],

modeling her custom-made ermine hunting outfit in preparation for an expedition to the Arctic . . . . Careless in the crook of her arm is a rifle with a power scope. Behind her on a wall . . . is an enormous moose's head, stuffed, upon whose nose someone has jauntily stuck a pair of sunglasses that are the exact copy of the Duchessa's—how truly conquered is that beast!

In a sense, civilization itself is conquered in this world. Its adventurers and warriors are purposeless, without a sustaining vision, without real objects on which to expend their energy. They can do no more than imitate the forms of the past, tame and domesticate Western Civilization, create parodies of the objects, ideas, and events that have energized Western man. In the passage cited above, not only is Venus vilified, but she is made a castrator, rendering a rifle into an impotent prop and an Arctic expedition into an excuse for a fashion display.

The place names, El Dorado, Fernwood, Arcadia, with which Oates has strewn her narrative,

suggest an ironic equation of suburbia with secular
paradise. Implicit in that equation is Oates's parody
of the American dream of an earthly paradise. Frederic I. Carpenter explains:

of . . . [the] ideas underlying the [American] dream, only
that of place has been wholly "American," for essentially
the dream is as old as the mind of man. Earlier versions
had placed it in Eden or in Heaven, in Atlantis or in
Utopia; but always in some country of the imagination.
Then the discovery of the new world gave substance to
the old myth, and suggested the realization of it on actual
earth. America became "the place" where the religious
prophecies of Isaiah and the Republican ideals of Plato
might be realized.[6]

That Oates is exploiting this aspect of the
American dream is apparent from Richard's assertion that Fernwood, the suburb in which he lives,
is paradise:

If God remakes Paradise it will be in the image of Fernwood, for Fernwood is Paradise constructed to answer all
desires before they are even felt . . . . Fernwood is an
angel's breath from heaven. It is as real as any dream,
more real than a nightmare, terribly real, heavily real . . . .
Fernwood is Paradise and it is real!

Nada confirms Richard in her declaration, "*This* is
heaven, I've found it . . . ."

Oates depicts Fernwood as paradise in a very
real, though deeply ironic, sense. Paradise is a place
where all vertical movement ends. In paradise there
is no where to go, no further purpose to be achieved,
no desires to feel, no objects to be obtained, no territory to conquer, no truth to be discovered, no
beauty to be revealed, no vision beyond it; in sum,
it is a dead end. The aimlessness of Fernwood's
adventurers, in fact, the whole tenor of these expensive people's activities, suggests this sense of sub-

urban paradise. Oates could not have chosen a more appropriate metaphor to express, at the same time, the temerity, stagnation, and finally, the danger of this American dream. The fault, in this novel, lies perhaps not so much in dreaming as in the conviction that the dream has been realized.

Indeed, the world of Fernwood is a contracting, circular world, where there is an illusion of vertical movement, of what sociologists term "upward mobility"—which is our materialistic society's version of spiritual progress—but in reality there is only repetition. As the Everetts move from one affluent suburb to another, still more affluent suburb, they respond with disbelief and denial to the fact that their neighbor in Cedar Grove is also their neighbor in Fernwood. When Richard moves from Fernwood back to Cedar Grove, he finds Gustave has also moved there. Marvis Grisell, an active, exotically dressed divorcée from Cedar Grove, reappears in Fernwood and, after Nada's death, becomes the new Mrs. Everett. Mr. Everett sells his Fernwood house to a man named Body, and another "Body" inhabits a house in Cedar Grove. Just as there is a house in Cedar Grove that has no furniture, there is a house in Pools Moran (another community) with no furniture; the houses are just hollow shells that echo the hollowness of this kind of paradise.

Although this portrait of suburbia is an indictment, the least of its purposes is condemnation. For Oates, suburbia provides an instance, within the "penumbra of time and place and circumstance," of the nature of man's limitations. This intent is given voice by the excuser for this desultory paradise and its inhabitants, Flavius Maurus, "who believed that the only Good was in desire and not in act, since purity can exist only in the mind." When morality resides in right desire rather than right action, then the world is no longer the field of man's being. Yet it is emphatically in the world that Oates's characters live, and it is by their acts and not by their desires that she measures them. No one can doubt that Hofstadter, Nada, and Everett are driven by a desire—albeit egotistical and deluded—for the Good, not by deliberate cruelty, although cruelty is often the result of their attempt to realize their desires; nor can one doubt that suburbia is created out of a genuine desire for an earthly paradise, not out of intentional fatuity. But in the words of T. S. Eliot, "Between the idea and the reality . . . falls the Shadow."[7] For Oates this Shadow is swollen with man's limitations, and for her it is the proper subject of tragedy:

We need to ask what tragedy has dealt with all along—has it not been the limitations of the human world? What is negotiable, accessible, what can be given proper incantatory names, what is, in Nietzsche's phrasing, "thinkable"—this is the domestic landscape out of which the wilderness will be shaped. If communal belief in God has diminished so that, as writers, we can no longer presume upon it, then a redefinition of God in terms of the furthest reaches of man's hallucinations can provide us with a new basis for tragedy.[8]

Despite the ironic voice of the novel's narrator, the tragic import of the world that he depicts is not really mitigated, for what is Fernwood but an instance of the reach of "man's hallucinations," and is it not a paradise created out of man's limitations? In Oates, the ideal does not so much enoble man as point to his impotence.

The novel centers on the conflict between the two opposing dreams of its central characters: Nada's for freedom and Richard's for mother-love. Moreover, it is the first dream that converts what is the child's birthright to his mother's love into the impossible dream. In Oates's vision, freedom obviates love because in loving, we acknowledge the burden of our otherness. Nada is, in fact, described as a solipsist. Just as Don Quixote's social class has no place in his society, Richard's helpless love for Nada has no place in Fernwood, where everyone lives within his own hallucinations.[9] Oates often uses children or young adolescents as dual symbols of human impotence and idealism, emblems of human limitation, who are powerless to realize their dreams.

In a sense, this novel concerns Richard's refusal to be initiated into experience. He murders Nada to stop the inevitable initiation that would have occurred had he not acted. For him, one image of Nada will always be what she is to him at the age of eleven. He has stopped the process that would have deflated his ideal although he tastes bitterly of knowledge and experience before he finally acts. Nada had seemed to Richard an emanation of higher existence—in her role as beautiful woman, the avatar of Beauty; in her role as writer, the avatar of Truth; and in her role as mother, the source of Being and Love. She is a counterbalance to the inveterate and myopic philistinism of his father. Richard acquiesces in her unreasonable demands because he desperately wants to be worthy of her. He takes the sadistic entrance examinations for the Johns Behemoth Boys School. When Nada asks him to retake an I.Q. test to prevent a "degenerative process" from "setting in" because Richard scored lower than she did, he retakes it, scoring higher. He maintains his Quixotean idealization of Nada, even when she abandons him for adventures with lovers.

Yet in Oates's fiction, knowledge and time eventually expose the ideal as a deception. Through

a series of discoveries, Richard learns that Nada's
demands do not stem from a wish to lead him to a
higher existence, one worthy of her, but rather stem
from a wish to deny his existence, destroy the "impossible pressure" of their bond, so that she can free
herself from feelings of guilt and responsibility; he
discovers the "Nada" that her name betrays. First,
he learns from his father that Nada had seriously
considered an abortion when she was pregnant with
him. Second, ravaging the Records' Room at Johns
Behemoth, Richard discovers that in his first I.Q. test
he scored 153 and in his second, 161, alerting him
to the malevolence of Nada's demands. Then at the
library he finds Nada's story, "The Molesters," in
which a young girl retells the story of an incident
with a molester three times. Each successive retelling incorporates a more adult perspective, betraying the parental influence in the child's interpretation of her experience. At the third retelling,
what is, in the first, an innocent encounter becomes
malevolent. It is the adults in the story who deform
the innocent into the grotesque; the parents are the
more dangerous molesters. Richard interprets the
three adults in the story as the three faces of Nada,
and Nada in her three faces is the molester who
subjects her innocent child to her perversions; she
is the mother who tells the child that it has been
subjected to perversion; and she is the father who
is impatient with and insensitive to the child's pain.
After reading this story, Richard sends for a mail-
order rifle.

Finally, Nada openly disavows her maternal
responsibility to Richard in a passionate speech on
freedom, triggered by Richard calling her "mother"
instead of the usual "Nada": "I don't particularly
care to be called *Mother* by anyone. I don't respond
to it. I'm trying to hold my own and that's it. No

Mother, no *Son.* No depending on anyone else. I want you to be so free, Richard, that you stink of it." Here again, Oates takes up the question of freedom, and again freedom is seen as an evil, as a way of denying one of life's most basic relationships—that of mother and child. Nada's speech seems all the more cruel when we remind ourselves that Richard is eleven at the time and not eighteen. By having an adult protagonist as the spokesman for freedom— moreover, a mother whose freedom depends on a repudiation of the parental role—Oates is stressing that freedom is always a negation, that freedom inevitably involves betrayal, repudiation, and denial. We could sympathize—and in fiction we often have sympathized—with a child's wanting freedom from parental domination as a condition of the maturation process, but Nada's is a different order of freedom. It is an extreme form of selfishness, a severing not only of the bonds that connect her to her identity, but also of the bonds that connect her son to his identity.

Oates's characteristic technique for pointing to the limitations inherent in autonomy is to place those characters who want to be free in a climate of the urgently real. That is, she presents the idealist in the setting of a pressing, demanding, actual environment in order to create a judgmental context wherein the value of his aspirations may be measured. By juxtaposing Nada's romantic quest for freedom with Richard's more compelling quest for his mother's love, Oates reduces the sense of urgency usually associated with quests for freedom. As Nada declares, "There is nothing personal, never anything personal in freedom . . . ." And it is just this cold impersonality implied by freedom that Oates is intent on revealing. At one point, Richard muses that the memoir could have been subtitled *Children*

of Freedom, and indeed the children in the novel,
many of whom are underdeveloped physically and
overdeveloped mentally or who are alcoholics or
dependent on drugs and psychiatrists, are "of freedom" in that they have been denied a protective,
nurturing parental love.

However, Oates portrays Richard as an idealist
who cannot accommodate himself to the real as well.
As the child who claims his right to his mother's
love, the character of Richard criticizes the striving
for freedom, but as a character who desperately
wants to capture and hold the romantic ideal that
Nada represents to him, Richard is yet another of
Oates's deluded romantics.

Oates depicts Richard's battle to capture Nada
as a battle against knowledge and against time. It
is only after attending a lecture on adolescent sexuality that Richard goes on his first sniper expedition, suggesting his inchoate fear that his sexual
awakening will corrupt his idealized love for Nada;
that the complexities of adulthood will invalidate
his innocent child-vision of Nada, the kind of vision
the girl in "The Molesters" has before her parents
defile her experience with their adult interpreta-
tions. Richard writes, "My kingdom was the place
we were going to enter finally, Nada and I. Together. Time was passing us, like a gentle spring
breeze that has come from some innocent cove thousands of miles away, and overtakes us, and passes
us by. I had to get us safely into that kingdom."
Richard attempts to enter his kingdom through
Nada's death; by causing her death, he believes that
he has finally established an irrevocable bond between them. By killing his mother Richard has en-
deavored to anesthetize himself against any further
revelations of Nada's betrayals, and, more impor-
tantly, to arrest the process of initiation, the process

that would have led him to emotional independence from Nada. He has attempted to protect himself from knowledge and to restrain the inexorable process of time. The kind of logic he employs to solve the conflict between his love for Nada and his impending initiation is the kind he employs in obtaining solutions for math problems: "My mathematical steps were always sensible, though my conclusions were often wrong. It was as if, led to the brink of the inevitable, my pencil somehow swerved and whimsically snatched at the impossible answer."

Oates often associates adolescence with romantic aspirations. Karen's growth into womanhood depends on her surrendering such aspirations. Jules and Maureen, the adolescent protagonists of *them,* become adults when the reconcile themselves to ordinary lives, to marriages and jobs. Richard never becomes truly "adult" because he has refused such a surrender, such a reconciliation.

Yet the final ironies with which Oates ends the novel are that Richard's act has neither shielded him from further betrayal nor shielded him from becoming "free" of Nada. Nada's last and most devastating betrayal follows her death. When Nada's parents attend her funeral, Richard discovers that she was not the exotic Russian expatriate writer, Natashya "Nada" Romanov she postured as, but that she was born Nancy Romanow, of a poor family in North Tonawanda, New York. Richard, like all the expensive people in this novel, has been pursuing his own hallucination. Moreover, no one recognizes the terrible intimacy he has established with his mother by becoming her murderer; no one believes his confession. Thus he is doomed to literally live out a "life sentence of freedom." In Oates's fiction, freedom is often imaged as an imprisonment, and perhaps Oates's most haunting image of this paradox is conveyed through Richard, who states, "You could inhabit the vacuum of your freedom like a fly buzzing aimlessly in a locked car, and not worry about getting out or about what you should be doing since you couldn't do anything anyway until you did get out."

Finally, the novel ends on a note of pathos, not tragedy. Heroes neither weigh 250 pounds, nor inhabit suburban worlds populated mostly by eleven-year-olds. In fact, Oates's intention in creating Richard may have been partially to parody the traditional hero. Perhaps we ought to take seriously Richard's assertion that he is "Hamlet stunted at eleven years of age." Richard's bulk may be a comic correlative of heroic "stature." His quest to win his mother's love may be a comic diminution of classic heroes' quests. And the fact that "Nada" turns out to be "Nancy" after all, that the ideal so ardently pursued is an "hallucination," may be an ironic illustration of Oates's belief that the ideal pursued by tragic heroes leads inevitably to a confirmation of human limitation. Oates's novels do not provide the relief we associate with the final act of tragedies, in which the old, corrupt world falls so that a new and better world may replace it. In her novels there is no old world to be redeemed and no new heaven and new earth to be gained, as her portrait of suburbia demonstrates. There is only *this* world. And it is toward this single, painful perception, the implications of which she repeatedly mines, that Oates's art so gracefully moves.

5

Shakespeare's Horatio as the Type for Joyce Carol Oates's Representative Man: *them*

In contrast to American romantic literature, Joyce Carol Oates's fiction is a fiction documenting the art of compromise, though not all of her protagonists—Shar, Swan, Richard, for example—are able to compromise. The inevitable return to the ordinary, the lessons on the art of compromise are perhaps two of the distinguishing characteristics of Oates's fiction. Success or failure, transcendence or doom, affirmation or denial do not describe the choices inherent in her fiction. Rather, in her fiction, compromise—which is both success and failure, but which is neither transcendence nor doom and which includes denial in its affirmation—is the only choice available outside of death or madness. Perhaps its most compelling feature is that it requires the individual to have a firm grasp on his selfhood, to have the ability to control his existence with a self made strong through compromise. Karen's survival is assured by her ability to meet these requirements; Swan's failure is due to his inabilities in this respect. Richard is arrested somewhere between the final postures of Karen and Swan.

In these early novels, however, compromise is the aftermath of a beloved's death, in one sense a submission to the impossibility of sustained love:

Karen loses Shar; Clara loses Swan; Richard loses
Nada (in each of these cases, the word "loses" could
be replaced by "murders" without much distortion).
Compromise is the only alternative after romantic
overreaching has led to the destruction of what is
most dear. Lowry and Karen fall into the ordinary
after their romantic aspirations are destroyed; but
in *them* (1969), *Wonderland* (1971), and *Do With Me
What You Will* (1973), the protagonists, Maureen,
Elena, and to an extent Jesse, in the end come to
be greedy for ordinary survival, for ordinary marriages. In the earlier novels, survival is the anticli-
mactic resolution after love alone fails to sustain life.
Karen's love for Shar must be relinquished in order
to sustain her selfhood; Swan's love for Clara is an
insufficient base for his existence; Richard's love for
Nada is endangered by an encrouching adulthood.
In these books, the characters who survive, who are
not absorbed by death like Swan and Shar, have
outlived their greater destinies and what follows is
a shadow existence.

Beginning with *them,* however, the climax occurs almost at the moment the central character re-
signs himself to ordinary existence. The moment
Jesse (*Wonderland*) leaves Reva Denk for his wife
and daughters, the moment Elena (*Do With Me
What You Will*) decides to leave Marvin Howe for
Jack, and the moment Maureen (*them*) decides that
she will marry Jim Randolph, these characters, by
falling back into the limited but real world, achieve
their destinies. In these stories, the *telos* of life is
not transcendence, not freedom, not wealth or
power, not even love, but a subservience to the life
process itself in which, for Oates, the ultimate meaning of human existence lies.[1]

Oates's representative man is not the hero, not
the Faustian overreacher, but Adam, or to put it in

the terms which Oates herself employs, he is not Hamlet but Horatio or Cassio or Kent. For Oates the man who is equal to history does not, like Hamlet, stand above it. Oates expresses this idea, which is central to *them*, through the voice of Jim Randolph, who, like Oates, teaches English. Leafing through *King Lear*, Randolph muses on the characters in Shakespearean tragedy: "A sense of apocalypse followed by an ordinary morning. Horatio and Fortinbras playing chess in a drafty, velvet-hung room, yawning and patient, good men left over to fight a good fight, ignorant enough to survive. And there was always a Cassio left over, bruised but energetic, and Kent, dazed with the past but optimistic enough to take on the future, the long rise of history." The center of gravity in Oates's fiction is not "in the sense of apocalypse" but in the "ordinary morning" that follows it.

In *them* Oates creates a violent, indeed apocalyptic world, one that seems at times in the final stages of disintegration, punctuated by terrible cataclysms, and bursting with malevolent passions. But the machinery of the novel is designed to transport the characters who navigate through this world to that "ordinary morning."

Oates's emphasis, especially in *A Garden of Earthly Delights* and *them*, on the struggle between the individual and history, or society, or environment has led some reviewers to the estimation that Oates is working in the tradition of naturalism. For instance, the first two sections of *A Garden of Earthly Delights*, which describe Clara's rise from the poverty and sordidness of a migrant worker's life, prompted Elizabeth Janeway to write, "Miss Oates's approach to fiction is more like Dreiser's than that of anyone else I can think of,"[2] a view with which most reviewers agree. Yet this estimation is

belied by the "third" section of the novel, in which
Swan, who has wealth and power, nevertheless
feels disjoined from the world.[3] His alienation, as
has been suggested, is rooted in a condition more
profound than the condition of being poor and powerless, the condition in which the heroes of naturalism find themselves.

Writing of the contemporary novel, Ihab Hassan states that "Whatever the hero may now be a
victim of, he is certainly not, as he was in the Thirties, a victim of systems or facts."[4] Yet *them* seems
on the surface to be following this older tradition.
The main characters—Loretta and her two children,
Jules and Maureen—seem the victims of the system
of poverty and of incontrovertible facts in the form
of unexpected and usually violent events. After Loretta's brother Brock murders her lover, Bernie
Malin, she submits to the lust of Howard Wendall,
a cop willing to dispose of Bernie's body, and marries him. She settles into marriage, motherhood, and
a neighborhood, with the comfortable thought that
"she had come to the end of her life . . . and it was
a solid, good feeling to think that she would prob
ably live here forever . . . ." However, her sleepy se-
renity is rocked when Howard is suspended from
the force for accepting bribes from prostitutes. The
entire Wendall clan retreats from the city and moves
to dilapidated quarters in the country. Again, her
equilibrium is disturbed, this time by the outbreak
of World War II. Howard is drafted and she must
face the nagging of her mother-in-law alone. Unwilling to waste her youth and energy on the barren,
rural landscape and the spiteful and imperious Ma
Wendall, Loretta flees to Detroit, where she is arrested for prostitution on her second day in the city.
World War II ends and the entire family is reunited,
bound together by the system of poverty, in the

slums of Detroit. But, again, a fact disrupts even these diminished circumstances. When Howard is killed in an industrial accident, Loretta is left alone to care for their three children and her ailing, querulous mother-in-law by herself. Loretta remarries, but her virile, attentive lover turns into a drunken, bad-tempered, out-of-work slum husband, who eventually nearly kills her daughter, Maureen.

Facts and systems not only victimize Loretta but also create the extreme rhythms of her children's lives. After a chase, Jules is caught by a policeman, who—infuriated by the chase, his natural animosity toward slum kids raised to murderous proportions—puts a gun to Jules's head; the chamber is empty and Jules survives a beating. Jules is taken up by Bernard Geffen, a sweaty, rumpled, hectic wheeler-dealer in shady investments, who offers Jules a job as a driver and promises adventure, money, and a college education—only to discover Geffen in a sleazy muffler shop with his throat slit, a bloody butcher knife nearby. Perhaps the greatest "fact" of Jules's life is his love for Nadine, Geffen's wealthy niece. She escapes with him in a stolen car to the South, where she refuses his lovemaking and abandons him while he is in a feverish delirium brought on by the flu. After recuperating in the South, he returns to Detroit to work for his prosperous Uncle Samson. His rising star reaches its zenith when he accidentally rediscovers Nadine and sinks into the blind, fateful, violent passion of their lovemaking. But Nadine rebels against a passion she cannot understand, control, or justify by attempting Jules's murder and her own suicide—both fail. His astonishment at Nadines's act, which occurs at the height of their love, plunges him into despair, rendering him passive and apathetic until the Detroit race riot of 1967 shakes him out of his somnambulism. He

awakens to the fact that, again, a policeman is trying
to kill him; Jules kills the policeman instead.

It is the force of two events that shapes the fate
of the passive, perpetually frightened Maureen.
Each event nullifies Maureen's attempt at liberation
and plunges her, after the second event, into a
nearly irremediable depression. She is entrusted
with the class record book after her election to
homeroom secretary. The book represents her acceptance by the world outside her native slum and-
her ticket to what she believes is a quieter, more
orderly and affluent life. She reveres it as a magic
token of her distance from the sordid, noisy squalor
of her home, as an icon whose powers are liberating,
as an emblem of the fact that she will not be forced,
like her mother, into "a future in which she waited
in an apartment for a man to come back." Because
she has imbued it with such undeserved significance, the notebook's disappearance causes her to
feel that the "world was opening up to trap her" and
that she is so guilty that "never, never would she
be forgiven, there was no way out." Still desperate
to escape her circumstances, she comes to believe
that money can be the vehicle of her liberation. She
begins a secret life of prostitution, hiding the cash
in a book—ironically, *The Poets of the New World.*
Loretta's second husband, Pat Furlong, discovers
Maureen's surreptitious life and her hidden cash
and beats her into a nearly cataleptic state.

The specific "facts" of murder, accident, abandonment, prostitution, and beating, which victimize
these characters, are, according to Oates, characteristic of modern urban life. Oates wants us to believe
that the events plaguing the characters of *them* are
typical, real, normal to the flow of life in cities like
Detroit. She states, "All of Detroit is melodrama,
and most lives in Detroit fated to be melodra-

matic . . . ." Geoffrey Wolff reports that in the note accompanying review copies of *them,* Oates writes, "Gothicism, whatever it is, is not a literary tradition so much as a fairly realistic assessment of modern life."[5] In fact, in the author's note prefacing the novel, she insists that not only is there verisimilitude in the plot and characters of *them,* but that this novel is a form of history, based on the experience of one of her students at the University of Detroit, the "Maureen" of the novel. Oates tells us that her student's "remarks where possible, have been incorporated into the narrative verbatim . . . . Nothing in the novel has been exaggerated in order to increase the possibility of drama—indeed, the various sordid and shocking events of slum life, detailed in other naturalistic works, have been understated here . . . ."

Thus Oates seems to be following the tradition of writers like Theodore Dreiser, whose *An American Tragedy* was based on an actual murder case and who used verbatim testimony from the actual trial in the fictional counterpart. This preface and the surface naturalism of the novel invite comments about the novel like those of Guy Davenport, who compares *them* to the work of the naturalists.[6] They invite the false perception that this novel, like those of the naturalists, is concerned with the conflict between the social and the individual. Despite the author's preface and the epigraph from John Webster's *The White Devil* that reads, "because we are poor/Shall we be vicious," social criticism is secondary to the awesome existential drama that *them* portrays.

The book has an epic sweep, enclosing the historical period from 1937–1967, from the rise of Naziism to the Detroit race riot of 1967. The protagonists are affected not only by the culture of the urban

slum but by historical forces as well. Loretta re-
members the devastating effect of the Depression
on her grandfather's construction business; and of
course, World War II, the Roosevelt administration,
and the Detroit riot are also plot elements. Yet this
"dependence on the real events in the lives of real
people" functions as an anchor and a setting for the
drama at the novel's core.[7] Oates says about Jules,
"Of the effort the spirit makes, this is the subject of
Jules's story; of its effort to achieve freedom, its
breaking out into beauty, in patches perhaps but
beauty anyway, and of Jules as an American youth—
these are some of the struggles he would have
thought worth recording." We are a far distance
from Dreiser's hero Clyde Griffiths, whose story
perhaps exposes the desert upon which American
values are built, but whose despair centers merely
on an inaccessibility to social stature, whose struggles and crimes are meanly motivated, meanly executed, the gestures of an insufficient soul caught
in an insignificant fate.

To cite an example that demonstrates that
Oates is dealing with something other than naturalism: Jules is offered the chance to "succeed," in
a way that Griffiths had hoped to succeed, by his
Uncle Samson, but easily gives up this chance when
he meets Nadine. The initial Jules is a romantic, not
a naturalistic character. He is motivated not by the
hope for material acquisition, but by the hope for
transcendence by means of romance and adventure.
Oates locates her fiction very specifically, not in
order to indict the location, as do Dreiser and other
naturalists, but to express her acute understanding
that the epic, of which the novel is a form, always
concerns the intersection of the individual and
larger worlds.[8]

In *them* Oates portrays an extremely severe

world in which the intersection of the individual
and larger worlds becomes the scene of cataclysm.
Rather than describing an environment that will-
fully oppresses the poverty-stricken, Oates is describing a universe of pure accident in which contingency dominates. There seems to be no relationship between the characters' acts and the
events which shape their lives; no link between intention and result. Violent upheaval meets their
every effort to control their own lives. In this world
they are continually in danger of absorption. It is
a violently unpredictable world in which murder,
beating, accident, abandonment strike almost in
proportion to the individual's effort to transcend his
circumstances. Here, Oates is portraying the cosmos
itself as the enforcer of human limitation.

To the characters who populate *them*, the most
obvious method of salvation from a world that stubbornly resists their manipulation appears to be the
heroic stance, the essence of which is an assertion
of will, by which they attempt to rise above or refute
their condition, their fate. As in much of her fiction,
Oates begins by imitating the rhythm of romance.
In characteristic American fashion, Oates's characters combat their alienation by intensifying it, by
establishing themselves as apart from the rest of
humanity.[9] One method by which they intensify
their alienation is through violence. This violence
is the response of the powerless to their impotence.[10]

Consistent with the pattern she established in
her earlier novels, Oates portrays this assertion of
will as nihilistic. The murder of Loretta's lover by
her brother Brock, for instance, is a case in point.
Before the murder, in a typical brother-sister exchange, Loretta spots his gun and asks him, "What
are you going to do with that gun?" " 'I'm going to

kill somebody with it,' he said seriously." Certainly,
he does not tote the gun in readiness to avenge his
sister's deflowering. Rather, he needs simply to
"kill somebody" in order to assert his strength in
a profound rebellion against his impotence. When,
as a middle-aged man, lying for months in a hospital
with an undetermined progressively debilitating
illness, his lip slowly eroding, Brock one day simply
gets up and walks out. In these cases, Brock's response to his own impotence is a paradoxical assertion of strength. It is not a remedy for impotence,
but a rebellion against it.

Violence as a rebellion against impotence takes
on the dimension of a motif, and perhaps the most
forceful example of this motif is Nadine's attempt
to kill Jules and herself. James R. Giles has correctly
placed the affair of Nadine and Jules in the Western
romantic love tradition, but he has not adequately
documented the use Oates has made of this tradition
in her depiction of their affair.[11] Their love is the
helpless, fated love to which we are accustomed in
romantic stories and Jules submits to it gladly. However, Nadine, echoing Maureen, is not happy to submit to it: "A woman is like a dream. Her life is a
dream of waiting . . . waiting for a man . . . . She has
no choice." Nadine, at bottom, is molded by middle-
class values and cannot rise to the occasion of Jules's
love. She talks of "venereal disease," of having committed "adultery;" she wants to know if Jules thinks
her a "pig." Yet she cannot help walking through
the door of her dream to Jules, and though they both
feel "locked in a desire for fusion," they are "turned
back rudely, baffled."

This inability to transcend through love the singleness of the self perhaps indicates that Oates
shares with D. H. Lawrence the belief that, "In sensual love, it is the two blood-systems, the man's and

the woman's, which sweep up into pure contact and
almost fuse. Almost mingle. Never quite. There is
always the finest imaginable wall between the two
blood-waves . . . but . . . the blood itself must never
break, or it means bleeding.''[12] Lawrence offered
this statement as criticism of Poe's perverse love
stories in which the protagonist madly insists upon
total fusion with his loved one. Oates, like Lawrence, recognizes the deathly aspects of romantic
love in which the goal is oneness. The failure of
fusion in her story is another failure of the romantic
promise, pointing to human limitation, even the limitations of love. However, behind all of her dramas
in which romantic goals are defeated is an awareness that in this defeat, a defeat imposed by human
limitation, is our salvation. The achievement of
these goals, as Lawrence implies, would mean
death. Nadine, following the protagonists of Poe,
attempts to achieve fusion through death. First she
wants Jules to kill her. Jules feels that "she wanted
her blood spilled by him, but Jules . . . did not want
to be shaped out of the air by her violent imagination." Since Jules refuses to destroy her, she attempts his death. Nadine cannot live with the ambivalence of her conventional morality and her
helpless love; she cannot tolerate the ambiguity that
is life's perpetual predicament. She attempts to rise
above her ambivalence by imitating the final act of
the heroine of some imagined melodrama by using
a gun. Her attempt at heroism, at making of herself
and her lover an emblem of a romantic abstraction
fails. She does not kill; she merely wounds, and in
the discrepancy between romantic intention and
prosaic result, lies human limitation; in this case,
it is a limitation that saves.

    The motif of strength against impotence cul-
minates in the Detroit riot. We watch as an insipid

and irresponsible group of academics, who are plan-
ning the riot, lightly banter the politics of murder
and destruction. Yet after the initial impetus, the riot
takes on a life of its own—it becomes "a fire that
burns and does its duty"—transforming the impo-
tencies of powerless people into gratuitous destructive energy. Usually law-abiding citizens are transformed into thieves and murderers, intoxicated by
the stolen opportunity to assert their force against
a defeating world. In a world where the individual
is constantly faced with his limitations, violence
seems a seductive form of liberation.

In a review of *them,* Joanne Leedom writes,
"The quest in *them* is for rebirth: the means is violence; the end is merely a realignment of patterns."[13]
Although it is true that the end is "merely a realignment of patterns," Oates does not portray violence
as an authentic means toward rebirth. Rather, it consumes its purpose as it is spent. Jules, in a television
interview after the Detroit riots, echoes the words
of Vinoba Bhave: "I would like to explain to everyone how necessary the fires are . . . not . . . so that
things can be built up again, black and white living
together, no, or black living by . . . themselves—no,
that has no importance, that is something for the
newspapers or the insurance companies. It is only
necessary to understand that fire burns and does its
duty, perpetually, and the fires will never be put
out—." The nature of fire—of violence and of passion—is merely to burn, to consume itself. It is not
a means to some·end, to liberation or rebirth or to
a better world. The "fire" about which Jules speaks
is perhaps Oates's symbol for humanity's desire to
burst its earthly confines, to transcend the common
rhythm of mortality, a desire whose expressions are
passionate but gratuitous.

The cataclysmic energies that penetrate Oates's

fiction finally nourish the ordinary by pointing to
its necessity. Oates's comment on the lesson of tragedy, we recall, is "man's goals are fated to be less
than his ideals would have them and when he realizes this truth he is 'enlightened' . . . ." Although
the ideal in *them* is liberation, "the sense of apocalypse," the goal achieved, as we shall see, is "the
ordinary morning." Jules states the case another
way in his television interview: "The rapist and his
victim rise up from the rubble, eventually, at dawn,
and brush themselves off and go down the street to
a diner . . . . Passion can't endure! It will come back
again and again but it can't endure!"

Oates's three main characters—Loretta, Maureen, and Jules—do not seek liberation through
violence, but through an alternate romantic method,
the creation of a future self that will triumph over
the present. Underlying this belief is the illusion
that the future, unlike the present, can be controlled
by the individual. Oates portrays Loretta as an inveterate optimist. Even at her most pessimistic moments, she harbors only a short-lived feeling of regret. We first see Loretta at the age of sixteen. It is
August, 1937, and Loretta is primping in front of a
mirror because it is Saturday night, and she is in
love: "It was her reflection in the mirror she loved,
and out of this dreamy, pleasing love there arose a
sense of excitement that was restless and blind—
which way would it move, what would happen? . . . Looking into the mirror was like looking into the future; everything was there, waiting."
She shares her son Jules's confidence in the poten-
tiality of the future, but unlike Jules, she hopes for
an ordinary destiny, the destiny of the "hundred
girls," like herself, who had "curly hair flung back
over their shoulders."

Loretta enters the Saturday night street scene

thinking hopefully that "anything might happen."
Even when Loretta is most disgruntled with her life
as an overweight, impoverished, bored housewife,
she resists her condition with a hopeful projection
of the future: "I know who I am—I got a lot of things
to do and places to see and this isn't all there is in
the world! Not for me!" Characteristically, she asserts the "I" against the whole world.

Perhaps Oates's most loving portrait of a character who has outrageously romantic aspirations is
of Jules. Unlike his mother, who envisions a ma-
terially successful future, a future that will simply
rescue her of its own volition, Jules envisions the
future as the success of his spirit in overcoming the
limits of his earthbound self; moreover it is a future
that he compels with his will. In fact, in some passages, Oates depicts him as an aspiring Nietzschean
Superman. "What he would like . . . was not to be
a saint exactly but to live a secular life parallel to
a sacred life . . . to expand Jules to the limits of his
skin and the range of his eyesight." For Jules as a
boy and as a man, the larger-than-life figure is the
object of his aspirations. After reading the words of
Vinoba Bhave in *Time*, Jules thinks, "He had not
liked Jesus . . . . He, Jules, would be a better man,
or a least a cleverer man—why not all the kingdoms
of the earth? Why not?" Although expressed in appropriately more youthful terms, he shares Lowry's
brand of hubris, believing he is his own world: "So
long as he owned his own car he could always be
in control of his fate—he was fated to nothing. He
was a true American . . . . He was second generation
to no one. *He was his own ancestors*" (emphasis
mine).[14]

Oates points to the hubris in romantic notions
of autonomy through Jules's audacious image of his
life as a book that he is writing. The initial Jules

never allows his romantic aspirations to be qualified by his experience with the real world. "He thought of himself as a character in a book being written by himself, a fictional fifteen-year-old with the capacity to become anything . . . ." He believes that he has the "spirit of the Lord" within him, and he believes in his own special fate. He is the only character in the novel whose vision rises above facticity, who has a sense that life is "backed by music." Unlike Maureen, Jules's spirit enables him to withstand the violent, unpredictable assaults of life—his father's death, Maureen's catalepsy, Geffen's death, Nadine's abandonment, the abuses of policemen, nuns, doctors, and peers—but it is unable to withstand Nadine's final betrayal. It is this assault of the unpredictable, occuring at the brink of victory, that causes "the spirit of the Lord [to depart] from Jules."

With Maureen, Oates creates a portrait antithetical to that of Jules, but on a deeper level Maureen is simply an alternative embodiment of the belief that the world is limited to the self. Loretta and Jules invoke the refrain "anything might happen" to describe a future filled with possibility. Although Maureen echoes this refrain, for her it indicates a future filled with unpredictability, a future of which she is a victim. Maureen is paralyzed by fear, acting only in desperation, feeling in continual danger of losing her selfhood. Like Swan, Maureen struggles with and is unable to authenticate her selfhood. "Nothing lasted for long . . . . It was her fate to be Maureen; that was that. But the Maureen she was in the presence of that man she'd been with . . . did not last. It came to an end." Maureen feels that the characters in the novels she reads have more reality than she does. "Maureen, dreaming over them, could feel herself begin to dissolve into nothing, nobody, an eye in a head, a blankness."[15] However, her selfhood is not undermined by feelings of ambiguity like Swan, but by the unpredictable violence that seems life's perpetual threat. She repeatedly envisions cataclysms—earthquakes, fires, the leveling of cities. When she sinks into the vegetative blankness of catatonia, she imagines herself as having no reflection in a mirror: "A person, a girl, imagines the mirror will show no reflection to her. So she does not dare look. Her body has the hopeless feeling of having become a weight, a bulk . . . . It has no reflection, no face. A headless body." In assuming that her mirror image defines the limits of her existence, Maureen betrays an underlying narcissism, in which one's mirror image describes the limits of one's world.

In her second letter to "Miss Oates," Maureen relates her experience of reading a whole year's newspapers at one sitting. The experience terrifies her because as reflected in the newspapers, "one day has nothing to do with the next;" the world seems "out of control." She writes, "When I read the newspapers I feel that I am losing myself, my own self, Maureen Wendall, and becoming like the world itself, not knowing what will happen the next day and never ready for it."

The passage expresses Maureen's fear of becoming absorbed in the chaotic rhythm of history. It is distinguished from Jules's and Jim Randolph's assessments of that rhythm because it has excluded the fall back into the ordinary, for it is the ordinary, the normal tedium of a quiet life that seems unreachable to Maureen. Her situation is so extreme— she is so inhibited by her fears—that her search for the ordinary life becomes an almost herculean task, a testimony to the risks involved in mere existence. Her very survival is extraordinary, and her achievement of husband, house, and baby almost miraculous.

Against her obsessive fear of engulfment, Maureen posits "form," an idea that she discusses at length in her two letters to "Miss Oates." To Maureen form means attaining protective permanence and fixity, giving shape to one's life that would make it invulnerable to attack. She "waited for the day when everything would be orderly and neat, . . . and she too might then be frozen hard, fixed, permanent, beyond their [the world's] ability to hurt." Part Three of the novel begins with an echo of the beginning of Part One, in which Loretta stands before her mirror: "A girl in love is standing before a mirror, very still." This time Maureen is able to see her own reflection. However, the crucial and distinguishing feature of this glance in the mirror is that she sees her face as the means of passage into the world. "Nothing can bring her into life, into the world, except that face."[16] And although she has no time for "love to rise in her," "she would have a baby . . . to make up for the absence of love, to locate love, to fix herself in a certain place . . . ." The "ordinary morning" has dawned for her. Maureen now has a grasp of her being, and although the self she has achieved is narrow, she has, at least, survived into selfhood. To Jules's question, "Do you love your husband?" Maureen answers, "I'm going to have a baby . . . ." To a survivor, love is not the point.

It is perhaps the book's greatest irony and its major point that Maureen's salvation is a submission to the very life from which she once sought escape— "waiting in an apartment for a man to come back"— documenting how in this novel, as opposed to romantic American fiction, survival replaces fulfillment and initiation replaces transcendence.

Although Oates does not provide her characters with the means of liberation from the world, from contingency and plurality, she does provide them with weapons with which they can reconcile themselves to the world. The way in which the characters endure the cataclysms that mark their lives, the way in which they eke out their survival, is with the fragile but effective weapons of forgiveness and promises. That is, with the faculty of forgiving, they deal with the irreversibility of the past and with the faculty of making promises, they deal with the uncertainty of the future.[17]

Loretta is a vivid though shallow character. Oates uses her to prepare the way for the more urgent and compelling portraits of Jules and Maureen. Loretta's life proceeds in fitful cycles of forgiving the past and making promises for the future. She is a vulgar, sentimental optimist capable of cruelty because she is able to ignore the malevolent dimensions of any situation. The sheer force of her adaptability, which requires a blind selfishness, keeps her from the madness that was the fate of her mother and father. Her frequent explosions into anger and tears usually result in an accommodating forgiveness of the past and a renewed hopefulness for the future. Her lack of depth and sensitivity, her selfishness, are almost redeemed by her malleability, her capacity to adapt, to forgive and make (though not always keep) promises. She forgives Brock for killing Bernie; she forgives Howard for institutionalizing her father; she forgives Ma Wendall for her spitefulness; she forgives Maureen for breaking up Jim Randolph's marriage. She can forgive everything because she is nearly impenetrable. She is able to cut the sharp edges off her experiences and make them palatable. Her weapon against unpredictability is the promise of a better job, a better apartment, a better man, a better child, or a new hairsyle. She swims on the surface of life with rather easy strokes of forgiveness and promises, never really in danger of sinking.

It is through the character of Maureen that Oates portrays the redeeming powers of forgiveness and hope. Maureen, as opposed to her mother, finds it nearly impossible to forgive and make promises, and that is why she is in constant danger. Her almost pathological obedience and passivity are underlined with hatred and obsessive fears. Her growth into selfhood is marked by her gaining the abilities to forgive the past, to "undo" it so to speak, and to make promises for the future that she can keep. Her marriage to Jim Randolph represents her new ability to forgive all the nameless men in her life to whom she has submitted. Against Jules's warning in the final scene of the novel—"Don't forget that this place here can burn down too. Men can come back into your life, Maureen, they can beat you up again and force your knees apart, why not? There's so much of it in the world, so much semen, so many men!"—she posits the promise of her baby: "She was going to have a baby, she was heavy with pregnancy, but sure-footed, pretty, clean, married." She transcends her initial state of passivity and obedience, a state in which she felt in constant danger of engulfment, by recognizing in the mirror a being whom she could bind to the future by making her promises of wifehood and motherhood, and with this being she would attempt to ward off the unpredictable, the events described in Jules's warning that perhaps await her in the future.

James Giles sees the final Jules as "a calculating nihilist" who, if he makes enough money and wins Nadine, will win a "victory of vengeance and quite conscious lust, having very little to do with love.

Anything is truly possible for Jules now; the
nihilistic rogue has replaced the idealistic
rebel."[18]Although it is true that the final Jules is no
longer the idealistic rebel, there is simply no evidence to indicate that he has become the nihilistic
rogue. His killing of the policeman during the riot
represents his awakening to the fact that someone
has tried to drain his lifeblood, and his rebellion
against that fact is in proportion to the tumult of the
riot in which it occurs. Although Nadine does not
succeed in killing his body, she has managed to kill
his sense of himself as extraordinary; she has killed
the "spirit of the Lord" within him, so that up to the
time of the incident with the policeman, he is in a
vegetative state, unable to care or feel or raise desire
within himself. However, when his life is in jeop-
ardy, he instinctively rebels against his own dying.
Although he can no longer aspire to the state of the
Nietzschean Superman, he has enough will to project himself into a future, though this future may be
ordinary. In Oates the final fall of the romantic hero
is the fall that illustrates human limitation. Jules,
however, learns to compromise, learns to live with
limitation, before his final fall. This return to the
ordinary is prefigured by his thoughts earlier in the
novel: "It could not be possible that he, Jules, was
growing up into a man like every other man—that
there was no special skill in him, no grace or deli-
cacy, no destiny in proportion to his desire." Although this is his fear, it is also the destiny with
which Oates redeems him. His last conversation
with Maureen is replete with promises for the future: "I'll always think of you, and maybe when
I've done better, gotten on my feet, when I come
back here and get married—I want to marry her
anyway, that woman, the one who tried to kill me,
I still love her and I'll come back and marry her,

wait and see—when I come back, a little better off, we can see each other." These are the ordinary promises of an ordinary person—not of a "nihilistic rogue" or of a Nietzschean Superman—for a good job, for love, and for marriage.[19] Hamlet has yielded to Horatio. At the end of the novel the emphasis is not on separation, as Robert M. Adams claims, but on hope for the future; Jules and Maureen say good-bye so that they can enter their individual and probably very ordinary destinies.[20] If there is something sad in that, there is something of positive resolution in it as well.[21]

6

~~~~~~

The Journey
from the "I" to the "Eye":
Wonderland

Oates's *Wonderland* (1971), like Lewis Carroll's
Alice in Wonderland is a book about proportions.
In fact, Carroll's Alice books strongly influenced the
theme, structure and imagery of Oates's *Wonderland*.[1] Oates has expressed great interest in Carroll's
work and has taught *Alice in Wonderland* and
Through the Looking Glass in her classes at Windsor. She considers these two very misanthropic
works that ask the "valid and terrifying" questions,
"Is life really a game?" and "Is everyone cheating
but me?" "In Carroll," says Oates, "life is a chess
game; you eat one another in order to get to another
square."[2] Like Alice, Jesse Harte, the novel's protagonist, undergoes a series of metamorphic transformations in which he grows larger and larger.
After he is orphaned—Jesse is the only surviving
member of his family after his father murders the
entire Harte family and then commits suicide—we
see him in succession as an obese adolescent (physically enlarged), as a cold, brilliant scientist (mentally enlarged), and as a vampirish husband and father (psychically enlarged). In order to escape her
father's engulfing domination, Jesse's younger
daughter Shelley (her name suggests "shell"), tries
to grow smaller and smaller; she attempts to extin-

guish her selfhood, to free herself of it, by method-
ically dreaming over her past and "erasing" it.
Jesse's narcissistic self-aggrandizement and Shelley's nihilism represent their wish to escape the im-
pinging external world by substituting the self for
the world. Jesse strives to redeem his personal history and refute a contingent reality by becoming his
own world. Shelley, on the other hand, strives to
free herself from her personal history, not realizing
that her personal history is part of the intricate design of time and universal history from which she
cannot extricate herself except through death. Jesse
and Shelly suffer from a distorted sense of self; they
presume the absolute primacy of self. Their refusal
to acknowledge the world leads them to opposite
routes of narcissism and nihilism.

The question of proportion between self and
world is, perhaps, the major question of the book.
It is encapsulated in the idea of "homeostasis"—
signifying a state of equilibrium—the controlling
metaphor of *Wonderland*. As Alice emerges from the
rabbit hole correctly proportioned, the final Jesse
shrinks from an *uebermensch* to an ordinary, self-
questioning being, who, in the ordeal of rescuing
Shelley from death, in the act of expressing love
through this rescue, learns that he cannot be self-
contained, that the overflow of self to other is an
imperative of life. He achieves homeostasis, which,
in this novel, signifies the precarious but necessary
equilibrium between the self and the world.

In the same way that Alice's voyage through her
dream worlds is the voyage of a typical Victorian
imagination through a landscape which symbolizes
Victorian culture, Jesse's voyage in *Wonderland* is
the voyage of a representative American through the
symbolic landscape of American culture.[3] Jesse's
substitution of the self for the world is given an

explicitly American context in *Wonderland.* The anonymous *Times Literary Supplement* reviewer has rightly described Jesse as "the Everyman victim . . . of American history."[4] Like many of Oates's protagonists, Jesse is violently wrenched from family and place, rendered homeless and an orphan by the initial events in the novel. Thereafter, he nurtures his own autonomy rather than depending on the nurture of the world outside. As a result, his becomes a quest for self-creation rather than initiation. Fiedler writes, "How could one tell where the American dream ended and the Faustian nightmare began; they held in common the hope of breaking through all limits and restraints, of reaching a place of total freedom . . . ."[5] In this American spirit, Jesse follows a Faustian pattern replacing communal life with personal power. However, unlike the European Faust, who has to reject traditions and sympathetic alliances in order to assert the primacy of self, Oates's American counterpart has nothing to reject. Homelessness, the absence of a defining context, is a condition that has been often idealized in the American imagination. In Oates's world, this condition produces in the individual dreams of self-creation and autonomy, but no means of actualizing them.

This delusion of self-creation and autonomy vitalizes Oates's characters' reckless idealism, their doomed pilgrimages in search of freedom, love, control; this delusion motivates their repeated efforts to shape the future, and to discover a release from a sense of history. Nada, Karen, Maureen, and Jesse regard themselves as existing outside of history, a view which, I have noted, signifies their loss of reality, their condition of spiritual as well as actual homelessness.

Both Carroll's and Oates's works are, in one respect, ventures in the pursuit of identity in a capricious universe. In each of Carroll's works, Alice asks, "Who am I?" Alice loses her identity because in stepping into an alien world, she has lost perspective, lost the knowledge of the relationship between herself and her environment. In Oates's work, this lack of a defining perspective is fundamental to the mythos of American culture. Jesse and Alice, aliens in the world in which they find themselves, attempt to discern the rules by which it operates, but on the brink of discovery, the landscape metamorphoses, leaving them continually adrift.

In *Through the Looking Glass*, the landscape alters each time Alice makes a move across the chessboard of her dream world. In Oates's novel, the chessboard is American history from December 14, 1939 to April, 1971, encompassing the Depression, World War II, Kennedy's assassination, the Vietnam War, the beatniks, the rise in the importance of scientific technology, and the hippie drug culture. With each move her protagonist effects, the landscape shifts into another era of our history that he must confront before proceeding. Jesse's confrontation with his collective history is a condition of his final awakening into an acceptance of his otherness. Like the Alice books, *Wonderland* is episodic, structured by Jesse's encounters with figures who embody aspects of American culture in this time period and, perhaps more significantly, who also represent heretical philosophical solutions to the problems of existence. Moreover, each of Jesse's metamorphic transformations is an accommodation to or a rejection of the ideologies of these representative figures. The one element common to all of these figures is that they substitute, in one way or another, the self for the world. In Oates's novel,

American history continually repeats the drama of the isolated ego.

The novel's first book, "Variations on an American Hymn," opens with a scene from the Depression, which is, as I have suggested, Oates's emblem for American dislocation. The imagery in this scene conveys a sense of claustrophobia, signifying the economic pressures on the Harte family who are Depression victims, and chaos, signifying the dislocation such pressures cause. Jesse says, "The air looks as if it is coming apart—shredding into molecules of sand or grit."[6] He feels smothered by the crowded quarters of his house, his mother's fifth pregnancy, and his father's financial failure. Later, as his father drives Jesse home from work, his sense of chaos increases, anticipating his father's bloody act and his consequent homelessness: "There is nothing in [the] sky to give a form to the day . . . . It is all a blur, shapeless, a dimension of fog and space, like the future itself." When he enters his house, he finds it awash with the blood of his family, the result of his crazed father's Depression-motivated acts; the father intends to kill Jesse as well, but he escapes death—although his father succeeds in wounding him before he commits suicide—by jumping out of a bedroom window "into the dark" and into the burden of his freedom. As an orphan, Jesse is the emblem of Oatesian nightmarish freedom, which equates freedom with the loss of identity and with the loss of a sustaining world.[7]

The next phase of American history with which the novel concerns itself is really a glance backward to the time when American life was centered on the farm. When Jesse leaves the hospital, he is in the care of his grandfather, a farmer, who lives alone and shuns human contact. He embodies the American agrarian ideal in which nature is a sufficient provider and companion. But more important, he represents a solipsistic solution to the problem of living. Before the murders, his grandfather is described as moving "in absolute silence, alone, a kind of nullity in the midst of the green corn." His creed is "People should leave one another alone." Jesse and his grandfather have a "partnership of silence." After the murders, Jesse gratefully plunges into his grandfather's life, welcoming the silence and the sense of objectivity the land imparts. He devotes himself to the rhythm of "sleep, waking, work" so that "he would not have to think about his life" that "would pass like this, one day after another . . . ."

However spring awakens Jesse's memory, and he asks to see his family's furniture, which is stored in his grandfather's barn. Jesse hungers for evidence of his own history, represented by the furniture, but his grandfather refuses to open the barn; he refuses to yield to Jesse's need to come to terms with his past. For the solipsist, this need is a violation of the terms of existence. Betrayed by his grandfather's stubborness, Jesse makes his way back to his father's deserted house, dreaming back over his life as he goes, repeating, *"I'm here, I'm here, I'm here. Jesse Hart is here, a survivor."* Oates's homeless protagonists are reduced to viewing mere survival as a triumph, a victory. In order to renew contact with his roots he spends the night in his empty, boarded-up house. The "Closed" sign his father placed on the property on the morning of the murders has been exchanged for a "For Sale" sign, an exchange which represents at the same time Jesse's survival, his orphaned state, and the prospect that he will have to find new connectedness for his selfhood.

After an interval in which Jesse spends a short time in his cousin Fritz's home and in an orphanage,

the novel shifts to the time of World War II. Jesse
is adopted by Dr. Karl Pedersen, an obese, obsessive, morphine-addicted surgeon and self-proclaimed seer who declares that war is "the very
heartbeat of life." A grotesque embodiment of
Nietzsche's Superman, Dr. Pedersen is a figure in
whom Naziism found its justification. He is one of
a series of *uebermensch* figures in Oates's fiction,
all of whom believe in the self as the final authority.
They are gluttonous overreachers portrayed as extremely fat, like Max in *With Shuddering Fall*, outrageously wealthy, like Marvin Howe in *Do With
Me What You Will*, and power-mad, like Andrew
Petrie in *The Assassins: A Book of Hours*. Their
obesity, wealth, and spiritual deformity imply the
extremest form of individualism, of what Quentin
Anderson has termed "secular incarnation."[8] They
melodramatically suggest the consequences of the
cultivation of absolute self.

Perhaps no other figure in Oates's fiction illustrates "secular incarnation" as well as Dr. Pedersen.
He declares that his specialty is "correcting defects
of nature, modifying certain freakish twists of fate."
He repeatedly states that his fate is to "displace
God." Concomitant to the idea of the absolute self
is the idea of perfection: *"Perfection is difficult,
but . . . not as difficult as imperfection."* In his the-
ology, death is a "surrender," not man's implacable
destiny. Dr. Pedersen is less a philosopher than a
theologian envisioning his own apotheosis. Jesse
becomes his dutiful proselyte, answering Pedersen's question, "How do you, Jesse Harte, intend to confront the riddle of existence?" with
"By . . . going as far as I can go, as far as . . . my
abilities will take me . . . ." Jesse's answer is the
promise each American boy makes to himself, a
promise sanctified by the Declaration of Independ-

ence, a promise, too, that ignores man's contingency, human finitude, the limitations inherent both in himself and the world in which he seeks to keep this promise. In the Pedersen household, the attempt to keep this promise leads to obesity, freakishness, deformity, and the love of war. Every member of the Pedersen household is fat, including Jesse, obesity being the physical correlative of megalomania. All of the Pedersens are crazed by an obsessive hunger, attempting with their expanding waistlines to fill space, to possess the world with their own physical being.

The episode with Dr. Pedersen concerns itself with freaks, which were no doubt suggested to Oates by the strange characters who populate Carroll's books. But perhaps more to the point, the condition of being a freak, of being deformed, is an extreme form of individualism, implying "a freedom in the very intensity of being."[9] Pedersen is a collector, and promoter in his own family, of freaks. He adopts Jesse because of the unusual way in which Jesse was orphaned. He maintains a "Book of Im personal Fates" that contains clippings from accounts of bizarre accidents. Among his collection of freaks, he numbers his daughter Hilda and his son, Frederich, whose respective skills in mathematics and music do not suggest genius so much as freakishness, deformity. In fact, they cannot manage simple hygienic routines like brushing teeth or changing dirty underwear.

The radical imbalance between self and world, which Dr. Pedersen and his family exemplify, an imbalance serving the grotesque aggrandizement of the self and leading to the exaltation of deformity, is countered with the idea of "homeostasis," which is first articulated by Jesse at the Pedersen dinner table:

The living being is an agency of such sort that each disturbing influence induces by itself the calling forth of compensatory activity to neutralize or repair the disturbance . . . . *The living being is stable. It must be so in order not to be destroyed . . . . by the colossal forces, often adverse, which surrounded it . . . . It is stable because it is modifiable—the slight instability is the necessary condition of the true stability of the organism.*

Equilibrium and modifiability are the key factors in the maintenance of homeostasis, factors conspicuously absent from Dr. Pedersen's ideology.

Although Jesse has memorized the definition of homeostasis, he does not achieve this condition until the last page of the novel. His willing absorption into the Pedersen household has precluded homeostasis. When Pedersen shows Jesse the headline, "Boy Eludes Gun-Toting Father," he rejects it, feeling that it "had nothing to do with him." Moreover, when he meets his cousin Fritz, who is a soldier about to enter World War II, he speculates that "if [Fritz] dies in the Navy there will be one less person to know me the way I used to be. . . ." In denying his past and not accepting it as part of himself, he has violated the law of homeostasis, which requires that one adjust to pain. He lives severed from his past and thus out of the normal continuum of time.

Irving Malin, in his essay "The Compulsive Design," notes the pattern in which many American protagonists "construct a design—a pattern to master their environment—but it becomes an inflexible measure which eventually destroys the self."[10] These "compulsive designers" are usually the heroes of American fiction according to Malin, but in

Oates, they are either the villains, like Pedersen, or the uninitiated, like Jesse. Following the pattern Malin describes, Jesse continually projects himself into the future, compulsively designing his future self, because he, for all practical purposes, has no past with which to substantiate his present self. He has only the projected Jesse of the future to confirm his existence.

However, Oates does not allow Jesse, the novel's hero, to capitulate totally to the imperatives of Pedersen's philosophy. Although he has tried to obey these imperatives because with his obedience has come the protective circle of a home and family, there is something in Jesse that responds to another's helplessness. It is this saving attribute that eventually redeems him. When Mrs. Pedersen tricks him into arranging her escape from her husband, he is reluctant, but he helps her. The attempt, of course, is futile and ends with Dr. Pedersen's declaration that Jesse is "dead" to him.

Oates describes the episode of Mrs. Pedersen's escape with cartoonlike exaggeration, doubtless inspired by Carroll; the cartoons become more and more extravagant as Mrs. Pedersen's and Jesse's predicament becomes more desperate. We see these two distraught, obese figures waddle luggageless into an elegant hotel. We see a panting Jesse drive back and forth from the hotel to the Pedersen home for more and more of the useless possessions Mrs. Pedersen—who cannot quite sever the umbilical cord that connects her to her home—desperately insists on having. We see them devour bag after bag of "take-out" Chinese food, their hunger the size of their fear. Before Jesse opens the note in which Pedersen declares him dead, he enters a fast-food place in order to stem the "tears of hunger [that] dimmed his vision." "Jesse settled himself carefully on one of the stools and ordered six hamburgers with chili sauce on them, three side dishes of French fries, and a Coke . . . . There was a shrill hunger in him that rose like a scream . . . ." His hunger is an externalization of his loss. He is hungry for the nourishment of home and family from which he has been orphaned for the second time, once at the age of fourteen and now at the age of seventeen. Jesse's compulsive substitution of food for loss is a paradigm of his future behavior pattern.[11] Although he no longer overeats, he will attempt to fortify his selfhood in other ways, first by expanding mentally—he becomes a brilliant neurosurgeon—and then by expanding psychically—he tries to possess his family. These are attempts to substitute the self for the world in order to become invulnerable to loss and defeat.

When we next encounter Jesse, as a young man, he is a student of medicine at the University of Michigan; the episode opens Book Two, "The Finite Passing of an Infinite Passion." His mentors during his medical studies are Dr. Cady, whose daughter, Helene, he marries, and Dr. Perrault, whose position as head of neurosurgery he acquires. They embody America's obsession in the 1950s and early 1960s with science as the way in which man can control his world. They offer empiricism and behaviorism as the ultimate philosophy and psychology. Dr. Cady compares the human body to a machine. He believes that our senses are our only access to reality, that ultimately, "*the world is our own construction.*" Dr. Perrault instructs Jesse that "the personal self and the soul are sentimental notions" and that "personality is an illusion . . . a tradition that dies hard." These theorists who reduce man to a machine, who deny the mysterious and manifold, relegate them to the status of mythology, are asserting their own power over existence. If the human brain is merely a matter of "mass, weight, substance . . . no miracle in creation," then as scientists, they are in complete control. As Jesse absorbs these lessons, his sense of control is heightened, a sense that is "pure, impersonal, brute."

As she takes her hero through American history, Oates exposes the various forms in which the self is substituted for the world: Jesse has confronted his nihilistic father, his solipsistic grandfather, the megalomaniac Pedersen, the empiricist Cady, and the behaviorist Perrault; yet the forms are not exhausted. Opposed to the heresies of empiricism and behaviorism are the antithetical heresies of Manichaeanism— a belief in the opposition of spirit and matter—whose avatar is Monk, a onetime medical student turned beat poet, and sensualism, whose avatar is Reva Denk, a kept woman whom Jesse first encounters while treating her lover after he castrated himself. Monk, known to his friends as Trick, believes that "man is a mouth and an anus," and thus the ultimate cure is the "separation of the spirit from the flesh." It is Monk, though, who accurately assesses Jesse's motives in his medical studies, stating that "Jesse aspires to a condition of personal bloodlessness" and that he wants *to raise the dead.*" Trick correctly gauges Jesse's drive to become a top neurosurgeon as a drive to insulate himself from the rest of humanity by becoming Christ the healer, by raising the (near) dead in removing their cancerous tumors. However, Jesse is a failed Christ because he cannot cure all humanity of its mortality. Medicine is finally dissatisfying; the cancerous tumors are infinitely more prolific than his ability to remove them.

Although, as we shall see, Oates portrays the final Jesse as Christlike, he has yet to reject sensual love, which the dream woman Reva Denk offers him as a means of escaping the pluralistic world. His infatuation with Reva releases him from a dependence on science as a means of controlling reality, but the fact that she represents just another guise of the self-enclosed ego is apparent to an Oates reader from the terms she sets for accepting Jesse's love: she forces him to vow never to see his wife and daughters again. While he prepares for their reunion with a ritualistic cleansing of his body, he studies his face in a mirror: "It was a curious terrain of slopes and ridges, skin and cartilage and freckles and small veins and hairs, brute dark hairs, pits, bumps, hollows." This examination leads to a moment of recognition, an epiphany, reminiscent of a similar moment that Roquentin in Sartre's *Nausea* experiences.[12] Unlike Roquentin, who abandons the world for the self, Jesse abandons self-indulgent sensuality for his responsibilities to his family and patients. Reva Denk, as her name suggests, represents all "dream-thinking," which must inevitably be relinquished for reality. With a razor blade, he hypnotically makes numerous cuts on his body, performing a ritual of purgation, an act that initiates the process that will cleanse him of narcissism and repair the rift between Jesse and the world. "Bleed ing" is an image of humanity; the previous Jesse, we recall, aspired to a condition of "bloodlessness." In the final cut, "he drew the blade through the tangle of pubic hair . . . ." This gesture of self-castration reminds the reader that the first time Jesse encountered Reva was when he treated Reva's lover after he had castrated himself. Thus Oates, in a curious and telling reversal of our expectations, associates Reva Denk, "dream-thinking," with castration, demonstrating once again Oates's antiromantic orientation. This act of self-mutilation and, strangely, of self-purification, ends Book Two, in which the "infinite passion" from which Jesse suffers, the passion that the self can control reality or get beyond it or that the self *is* reality, submits to a "finite passing."

With Jesse, Oates has created a Faustian character who makes pacts with modern devil figures— grandfather Vogel, Dr. Pedersen, and Dr. Perrault, and although he has rejected these figures, he must, like Faust, still win salvation, which in Oates does not mean a place in heaven, but rather a place in the world. Although Jesse leaves Reva for his family out of an inchoate awareness that his authentic selfhood is substantiated by the bonds and the web of responsibilities inherent in family membership, he wrongfully assumes that he *is* his family, that by possessing them, by absorbing and assimilating them, he can render them and thus himself inviolable. His wife, Helene, complains, "He wants to be us . . . . He wants to own us . . . ." This effort to control and dominate indicates that Jesse's consciousness is still clouded by the delusion that the self is the world. Baffled by his failure to establish himself, he compulsively writes the word "homeostasis," as if to achieve this state through incantation. Taking a walk, Jesse "circles" his house, "a circle that must have taken him five miles, the house remaining in its center, in the very center of his consciousness, his wife and daughters sleeping in the center . . . ." Thirty years after his father orphans him, he is still attempting to reenter the sanctity of home and family, to re-create those violently severed bonds.

The last episode in American history that the novel treats is that of the hippie drug culture, which takes up Book III, "Dreaming America." It is structured largely by the letters that Jesse's runaway daughter, Shelley, writes to him. She is under the influence of Noel, the last devil figure in the novel. Noel is a figure out of America's 1960's. An apostle of nihilism, he preaches an absolute denial of ego, of history, of existence. He says, *"We are all becoming extinct."* By becoming Noel's proselyte, Shelley is countering the tyranny of her father's narcissism. Shelley strives for freedom in self-extinction: "I want darkness, the flow of blood without bubbles of oxygen or memory, I want to be free of you [Jesse] . . . ." Despite her effort to oppose her father with a quest antithetical to his, she is engaged in a similar effort because narcissism and nihilism are alternative quests for autonomy and freedom.

Shelly's rejection of Jesse strikes at the very root of his inadequacy. His myth of control is dissipated by Shelley's flight. As remedy, Jesse applies the only lesson he ever learned from reading fiction, that "love demanded rescue." As he makes his way through the crowded hippie community in Toronto, from which Shelley has written a veiled plea for rescue, Jesse rehearses all of the identities he has taken on and cast off: "Maybe even another Jesse here somewhere, hidden by the crowd, on the other side of the street, hunting . . . a perspiring, overweight Jesse, hurrying to keep up with this lean, anxious Jesse? . . . a scrawny, frightened young Jesse, hurrying along this confusing tide?" Tellingly, Jesse speaks of himself objectively, in the third person. Aware of the futility of pursuing these cast off selves, he seeks for yet another redeeming self: "Was there, in that shadow-ridden heaven, another form of Jesse too, watching him, yearning to draw up to him Jesse's hollow, radiant, yearning self? Yearning to purify himself at last, after so many years?" However, he tacitly renounces this ephemeral Jesse, renounces all of the objectively created Jesses, with the gesture of throwing his clothes and his wallet, containing all of his identification papers, into a garbage bin in order to proceed with the more urgent task of Shelley's rescue.

The first edition of the novel (1971) ends differently than all subsequent hardcover and paperback editions. Although Jesse rescues Shelley from Noel, this edition ends on an ambiguous note, with his still pursuing "the true, pure, undefiled Jesse."[13] The focus is on Jesse rather than on his redeeming act as it is in the subsequent editions. Oates has said that the revised ending, which came to her in a dream, is the one she prefers. We can be grateful for the revision since the closing sequence of the first edition seems to violate the intrinsic movement of this carefully structured novel.[14]

In the authoritative edition, Jesse brings the gun he purchased in recoil against President Kennedy's assassination to Noel and Shelley's room, but when he arrives, he vows, *"Nobody is going to die tonight . . . . Not on my hands."* Thus, instead of repeating his father's act, he redeems it, and in so doing, he recovers his lost identity. As Jesse leads Shelley away from Noel, she says to her father, "You are the devil . . . come to get me to bring me home . . . ." However, Shelley is mistaken. Satan, as Milton saw, deludes man with the promise that he can be equal to God. Paradoxically, by denying his daughter freedom, by forcing her back into the limitations of time and history, to the ironically nourishing restrictions of life lived within the bounds of family and place, Jesse finally becomes the redeeming Christ who acts on the imperative that "love demands rescue." As Alice successfully moves across the chessboard to become the white Queen, Jesse has moved across the chessboard of American history to become kingly.

Oates further associates Jesse with Christ in

that in addition to his being a healer whose redeeming act is an act of rescue through love, "Jesse"
signifies the genealogical tree that represents Christ's
genealogy. However, the novel also contains some
perversions of Christian figures. Dr. Pedersen, for
instance, suggests St. Peter, but the church he
builds is on the rock of gluttony and megalomania.
Further, when Jesse enters the Toronto apartment
in search of Shelley, Noel (the name is itself a pun)
identifies himself as St. John. Yet the revelation of
this ersatz prophet is of a new heaven and new earth
in which humanity will be extinct. Thus when Shelley accuses Jesse of being Satan, she is using the
vocabulary of this perverted universe, a universe
that Jesse redeems. Jesse answers Shelley's accu-
sation with the question, "Am I?" The reply is a
declaration of existence, a question that reveals his
recognition, too, of his contingency; it serves as an
answer to his former question, *"Jesse Vogel: who
was that,"* and it signifies that Jesse has finally
"entered his own history," has achieved the precarious equilibrium between self and world.

   The novel is organized by a complex structure
of imagery that reinforces the movement from narcissistic individualism to homeostasis. Probably inspired by the eating scenes and the fluctuating sizes
of characters in Carroll's works, Oates strews the
novel with images of mouths—and related images
of wombs, sacs, boxes, shells, and cells—and pictures of disproportionate human bodies. Jesse's father is pictured as continually "chewing and grind
ing." At the Pedersens', Jesse feels that "tiny
pinpricks, tiny sparks, seemed to be rushing from
every part of his body toward his mouth, concentrated most fiercely in the moist flesh on the inside
of his mouth." In addition, the Pedersens are usually pictured at the dinner table, where Jesse stud-

ies their "moving jaws." Jesse feels rage at the sight
of Trick's "moving mouth," and Trick writes a poem
entitled "Mouth." Helene, studying cell slides
through a microscope, describes the cells as "pure
mouth." In a gynecologist's office, she describes
"the raw reddened gap between her legs" as "a raw
demanding mouth." Jesse's image of Reva is the
"mouth with its perfect smile."

Through the oral imagery, Oates associates the
drive to substitute the self for the world with the
infantile consciousness. The mouth is the organ
through which the infant experiences pleasure and
through which it expresses pain. The demanding
infant depends on the external world for satisfaction, yet has no awareness of it, sees it as an extension of the self. His limited awareness allows recognition only of his own pain and satisfaction. The
mouth thus signifies a narcissistic apprehension, the
infantile consciousness before it has learned to dif-
ferentiate between itself and the world, suggesting
that extreme individualism arrests the natural maturation of consciousness.[15]

The image of the womb, especially the pregnant womb, has similar reverberations. Moreover,
the fetus in the womb imagery is sometimes a *doppelgänger* for the woman herself. For Hilda, Dr.
Pedersen's daughter, the womb is a place to which
she may retreat from her rapacious father. It is her
"secret space"; "In that small sac of a space where
a baby might grow, . . . she lived in secret" from her
family. Helene, too, is obsessed with her womb; she
is revolted by the biological process of pregnancy
to which she must surrender her body. She sees it
as an impersonal process: "It could have been said
of any woman, anyone at all." Helene, like all of the
characters in *Wonderland,* suffers from a disproportionate sense of self. The pregnancy violates her

integrity, intrudes on her singleness, and signifies her victimization by a process outside her control. Shelly, on the other hand, wants to drain herself out of her shell; she wants to regress into the cell, expelled by her father, from which she came. Characteristically, she imagines her womb as barren, writing to Jesse, "My belly is hollow . . . ."

The particular distortions of mouth and womb are part of a larger distortion of the entire human body. On the day of the murders, a drawing in the boys' lavatory catches Jesse's eye:

a woman's body seen from the bottom up, the legs muscular and very long, spread apart, the head at the far end of the body small as a pea, with eyes and eyelashes nevertheless drawn in very carefully so that they look real. Someone has added to the drawing with another, blunter pencil, making the body boxlike, the space between the legs shaded in to a hard black rectangle like a door. The arms have also been changed to walls and even the suggestion of brick added to them . . . ."

Jesse, fascinated by the drawing, feels, "It is something you could walk into and lose yourself in, all that empty blackness . . . ." A drawing of a closed box is superimposed on the erotic drawing of a woman's body, suggesting that the prisonhouse of self is a kind of auto-eroticism, meaningless ("empty blackness"), but absorbing ("something you could walk into and lose yourself in"). He sees a similar image in Mrs. Pedersen—whose body he compares to a coffin—when he forces the door of the bathroom in which she has locked herself and finds her on the floor, naked. These distorted images yield to an image of a body correctly proportioned that Jesse sees on another lavatory wall, minutes before he rescues Shelly: "a woman's cadaver, the heart and the lungs exposed, the stomach sac, coils of intes-

tines, the womb carefully drawn, Jesse found himself examining the drawing, surprised that it was so
good. The organs were in their proper proportions.
At the very center of the little womb was an eye,
elaborately inked in." In this drawing everything
is exposed, the body free, not imprisoned by walls
or a coffin. The fetus in the womb is an "eye," symbolic of Jesse's rebirth into a truer vision, into a
delicate balance between self and world in which
the narcissistic "I" has yielded to the "eye" whose
sight is bifocal, turned inward and outward at the
same time.

The poem, "Wonderland"—first published as
"Iris Into Eye," in *Poetry Northwest* (Autumn,
1970)—precedes Book One of the novel and is a
poetic encapsulation of the novel's movement. It
traces the evolution of life from inorganic atoms,
"spheres are whirling without sound inside/spheres,"
through the beginning of life, "the collapsible space
begins to breathe/the vertebrae lengthen into life,"
to the emergence of consciousness: "the eye wid-
ens/the iris becomes an eye/intestines shape themselves fine as silk/I make my way up through mar-
row/through my own heavy blood/my eyes eager as
thumbs/entering my own history like a tear/bal-
anced on the outermost edge/of the eyelid."

For Oates, the process of creation culminates
in consciousness, in the dual awareness of self and
other. She suggests that although it is a precarious
and painful condition ("a tear/balanced on the outermost edge/of the eyelid"), it is the only way to
enter one's history, to achieve one's own identity.
The poem treats in cosmic terms what the novel
treats in historical, cultural, and philosophical terms.

Wonderland is perhaps Oates's most ambitious
work. The novel's structure—the correlation of the
historical, cultural, religious, philosophical, and

psychological in the life story of one character—is possibly Oates's attempt to realize what she has called her "laughably Balzacian ambition to get the whole world into a book."[16] Of it, she said, "I couldn't do it again. It might be my last novel, at least my last large, ambitious novel, where I try to re-create a man's soul, absorb myself into his consciousness and co-exist with him."[17] She has taken her protagonist through major events in a thirty-two-year period of American history in which he encounters figures who offered violence, solipsism, megalomania, empiricism, behaviorism, Manichaeanism, sensualism, and nihilism as paths of truth in order to point to the redeeming path of love, which requires a recognition that the world is larger than the single ego.

7

Crime-Crossed Lovers:
Do With Me What You Will

As Oates suggests with the oral imagery, as well as
with the metaphors of obesity and freaks, in *Wonderland,* the romantic aspiration to house the world
in the self is an expression of the narcissistic consciousness. The drama of the self-enclosed personality, of the "introverted libido," that permeates
Oates's novels, suggests an affinity with Freud who
thought of the psyche as profoundly narcissistic.[1]
Freud argued that one of the deepest impulses of
the psyche is to overpower and incorporate the
world, to resist division into self and world.[2] Yet,
with Freud, Oates insists that division of self from
world is the essential nature of reality and that
health implies an adjustment to its demands. Indeed, Oates's dominant method of characterization
is deflation: those characters who begin as romantic
figures, who have a sense of themselves as limitless,
are at the end reduced to more realistic proportions.
In *them,* for instance, the characters' confrontations
with the fluidity and violence of American culture
have the effect of imposing sudden and startling
revelations of their powerlessness and dependency.
Oates's art is thus a highly structured mixture of romance and realism.

Nada, in *Expensive People,* provides an example of Oates's deflationary method of characteriza-

tion. When Richard describes his mother to us, he
presents a woman of exotic Russian ancestry, an
aristocrat-artist who is misplaced, demeaned, stul-
tified in American suburbia. She is a romantic figure
with whom we sympathize almost despite ourselves. But towards the end of the book Richard in-
forms us that she is not an aristocrat at all, but Nancy
Romanow, raised in upstate New York by dim and
beaten parents. Consequently, we feel as does Richard—tricked, betrayed; we feel that a person with
an ordinary history has no right to such postures, no
right to yield to the narcissistic impulse. Through
this sudden deflation, through Oates's sudden juxtaposition of Nada with Nancy, we are forced to confront the arrogance and cruelty of Nada's romantic
aspirations in the face of the prosaic but very pressing needs of Richard for mother-love and stability.

The movement of Oates's art is a relentless,
painful deflation, terminating in pathos, the dominant emotive charge at the end of each of Oates's
novels, a pathos comprised of loss, the loss of the
delusion of the self-sufficient ego, and of inevitability, the inevitability of the world. We remember
that Oates, in an unusually exhortatory statement,
has said, "the novelist's obligation is to do no less
than attempt the sanctification of the world," and
she does this in her fiction by painfully imprinting
the world on the consciousness of her protagonists.[3]
The epigraph to *Do With Me What You Will* from
Henry James may stand for most of the novels: "The
world as it stands is no illusion, no phantasm, no
evil dream of a night; we wake up to it again for
ever and ever; we can neither forget it nor deny it
nor dispense with it."

In *Do With Me What You Will* (1973) Oates creates her most controlled mixture of romance and

realism. For the first time in an Oates novel romantic love with fairy-tale precision (almost) conquers all.[4] However, in the course of conquering, love is besmirched by crimes of adultery, abandonment, and selfishness. Yet those very crimes paradoxically make the fairy-tale ending possible and transmute the fantasy into a realistic vision of the redeeming possibilities of love.

Indeed the fairy-tale element permeates much of the plot and characterization of the novel. There is the extraordinary beautiful, blonde-haired Elena, the pliant, passive fairy-tale princess, who is described as a "little doll," having a "dreamlike face," as "virginal," "perfect," the "Queen of Sleep," a woman "who is being dreamed." At the age of seven she is abducted and mistreated by her father, who is unwillingly divorced from her mother. He dyes her hair black and tells her that her mother is dead. He keeps her locked in a motel room where he starves her, sedates her with gin, and finally abandons her. When her mother, Ardis, picks her up at the children's shelter in which the police have placed her, Elena is autistic, finding if difficult to move or eat and impossible to speak.

Ardis, a version of the fairy-tale stepmother, forces her to speak by threatening to abandon her. She continues cruelly to manipulate her until Elena is seventeen, when Ardis arranges a marriage for her to Marvin Howe, an extremely rich and powerful lawyer whom Elena has seen only twice and who is twenty-four years her senior. The marriage is sealed with a contract Howe makes up, containing forty-five clauses, none of which speaks of love, but one clause dictates that they will never have children.[5] Through it all, the good princess Elena feels only love for her oppressors as she sleeps through

"Twenty-eight Years, Two Months, and Twenty-six Days" (the title of Part I) of her life in a "virginal blankness."

In due course there appears a rescuing prince, another lawyer, Jack Morrissey. He awakens Elena from sleep—literally, she is in a cataleptic state—and after she shears off her waist-long hair, they escape together.

These fairy-tale elements are tempered by the realistic aspects of plot and characterization. The father, for instance, is not consciously wicked, but psychologically maimed, a result of a forced separation from Ardis that inspires his desperate, revenge-motivated abduction of Elena. Jack, moreover, is hardly the pure, stalwart, love-stricken prince. Aside from already being married, he is egotistical and inept, resolved to end the affair he has with Elena; but she, discovering a never-before-exercised aggression, practically abducts him and thus effects her own escape. In addition, the fairy tale is veiled by the frequent shifts from third-person narration to interior monologue that give the plot its strong sense of psychological probability.

In her discussion of the novel, Oates has emphasized that the lovers' union is guided by fate, that they really have no choice.[6] Though her comment is an exaggeration, a strong sense of inevitability is conveyed by the calculated symmetry of plot and structure, reminiscent of Henry James's *The Golden Bowl*, that amplifies and enhances the fairy-tale effect. Part I, "Twenty-eight Years, Two Months, Twenty-six Days," chronicles the history of Elena from May 4, 1950, up to the moment on April 12, 1971, in which Elena stands frozen, her watch stopped at 1:45, in front of the Alger Memorial in Detroit. Part II, "Miscellaneous Facts, Events, Fantasies, Evidence Admissible and Inadmissible," chronicles the history of Jack Morrissey from January 18, 1953, until the moment he brings her back to consciousness at the Alger Memorial. Parts I and II, moreover, both begin with a father's crime: Part I with Leo Ross's abduction of Elena, Part II with Joseph Morrissey's murder of Neal Stehlin, whom Morrissey blamed for his retarded son's death. The link between Elena and Jack is Marvin Howe, who saves them both. He saves Elena from the contemptible Sadoff, the man for whom Ardis works and to whom, before Howe appears, she plans to marry Elena. He also saves Jack by winning a verdict of not guilty by reason of insanity for Jack's father.

Oates strengthens the impression that these lovers are star-crossed by giving a sense of synchronicity to their thoughts and characters. For instance, both have similar feelings about the effect Howe has had on their lives. Elena thinks, *"Hurtled across the landscape, picked up in one place and set down in another."* At his father's trial Jack muses," *. . . as if an ordinary man were seized by a whirlwind, picked up and flung a great distance, and then left . . . ."* Indeed they use similar words to describe their decision to love one another. When Jack sees Elena in front of the Alger Memorial, he thinks, *"You'll do."* Elena, catching sight of Jack in the lobby of the San Francisco hotel where they plan to have their affair, thinks, *"He would do."* Both Elena and Jack are described as "invisible." As Elena is "invisible" behind her extraordinary beauty, Jack is invisible, hiding behind his lawyer's mask. In a heated moment, his wife, Rachael, accuses him of being an "invisible pimp" for the law.

Yet the sense that fate governs these lovers is deeply undercut by the countering metaphor of crime, which implies personal motivation and choice

realized in individual action. The novel is built on
the opposition between romance and realism; between fairy tales and life; between innocence and
criminality. Crime is the means by which Oates rescues Elena and Jack from their narcissistic insularity, for the possibility of crime indicates that there
is a world outside the self and that this larger world
can be affected by individual acts. Moreover, the
acceptance of criminality, of guilt, implies a profound recognition of otherness.

Part III of the novel is entitled "Crime" and
Part IV "The Summing Up." Thus all four titles
more or less correspond to the procedures of a trial.
On trial in this book are the very concepts of innocence and guilt and their respective counterparts,
law and love. Law and innocence are the novel's
metaphors for the undivided, narcissistic consciousness that believes the world is housed in the self,
and love and guilt are the metaphors for the divided
consciousness that accepts the world as separate
from the self. In Oates's portrayal, the law allows
the individual to declare himself innocent of his
responsibilities to the world, and love, the extension
of the self to the other, forces him to acknowledge
the world, to accept the burden of guilt and responsibility for his actions in the world. In this
novel the spiritual and psychological struggle is
between the composite monster Narcissus-Faust
and Adam, fallen man.

In fact, in 1973, the year *Do With Me What You
Will* was published, Oates published two articles in
which her pervasive disenchantment with the narcissistic "isolated self" mounts to moral rage. In
Psychology Today she writes, "The 'subjectivity-is-
truth' of Soren Kierkegaard and others is an out-
dated existentialism, which fails to see how the consciousness of any man *is* an objective event in na-

ture . . . . It is not the private possession of the
individual just as the individual is not 'his' own
private possession, but belongs to his culture."[7] She
ends the article with the statement, part of which
has been previously cited, of her own artistic purpose: "All the books published under my name in
the past 10 years have been formalized, complex
propositions about the nature of personality and its
relationship to a specific culture (contemporary
America) . . . . *Many myths must be exposed and
relegated to the past, but the myth of the 'isolated
self' will be the most difficult to destroy,* (emphasis
mine).[8]

In "The Death Throes of Romanticism: The
Poetry of Sylvia Plath," first published in *The
Southern Review* (Fall, 1973), she states:

Sylvia Plath acted out in her poetry and in her private life
the deathliness of an old consciousness, the old corrupt-
ing hell of the Renaissance ideal and its 'I'-ness, separate
and distinct from all other fields of consciousness . . . .
Where at one point in civilization this very masculine,
combative ideal of an "I" set against all other "I's" . . . was
necessary in order to wrench man from the hermetic contemplation of a God-centered universe and get him into
action, it is no longer necessary, *its health has become
a pathology, and whoever clings to its outmoded concepts
will die* [emphasis mine].[9]

In *Do With Me What You Will* this rage against the
"I" finds its objective correlative.

All of the major characters in the novel are man-
ifestations of narcissistic or Faustian urges, alternate
urges of the undivided consciousness. These American overreachers attempt to elude the world, to
elude history—Marvin through incorporation, Ardis
through manipulation, Jack through fantasies of control, and even Elena through the blankness into
which she retreats. But most of all in this novel

about law, they wish to elude guilt and thus, in the terms proposed by Oates, life. The following statement by Ardis is particularly revealing in light of Oates's comments on "I"-ness: "We're our own ideas, we make ourselves up; some women let men make them up, . . . but not me, I'm nobody's idea but my own. I know who I am." Ardis's statement signifies a narcissistic apprehension of life, an extreme assertion of self-reliance, that is predicated on a denial of reciprocity, a statement defending, justifying solipsism. Her assertion of complete self-knowledge suggests the rigidity and inflexibility, the finality, of a sculptor's creation, of a person who has closed himself off from process, clinging to a "compulsive design" of himself at the cost of love and relatedness. Indeed after a face-lift, Ardis finds that her grown-up daughter is an embarrassing refutation of her posture of youth, so she warns Elena that she must not acknowledge her as her mother. Like Nada (*Expensive People*), she is led to deny her child in order to maintain her fantasy. When she later declares her belief that "love is destructive of the ego," she reveals her diseased consciousness. In the words of Freud, "A strong egoism is a protection against disease, but in the last resort we must begin to love in order that we may not fall ill . . . ."[10]

In Marvin Howe, Oates has created a caricature, if not an allegorical image of America, a character who is bloated with his self-importance, a self-declared God whose greatest desire is power and whose deadly sin is greed. His megalomania and greed link him to Max, Clara, and Dr. Pedersen and to the suburbanites of *Expensive People*. Beginning as a poor, Oklahoma boy, Marvin realized the American Dream "of having a million before you're thirty" in the American way: "I knew what I was going to do, and I did it." He commands huge fees, exchang-

ing verdicts of innocence for all of his client's possessions. Having saved many people from death, he
feels that he is himself "immortal." Yet Howe, as
representative of American greed, is best dramatized in his voracious appetite to accumulate *things*.
Showing Elena through one of his immense ware-
houses, filled with the objects he has collected in
clients' fees, he says, "A great crowd of people with
money and time spent their lives accumulating
these things, and in a way I assimilate them, their
lives, simply by owning their possessions." Howe
attempts a literal incorporation of the world by accumulating as much of it as he can. Elena is herself
the "sacred object," the symbol of Howe's divinity,
corroborating his grotesque self-apotheosis.

Howe excuses his greed in the name of Law
just as Ardis excuses hers in the name of Beauty,
but these excuses are evasions, ways of making guilt
appear as innocence. In the end, Oates's portraits
of Ardis and Howe amount to a parody of the Faustian, heroic ego. In effect, she reimagines Faust as
he would appear in the godless present in which
heaven and hell can neither redeem nor condemn
him, nor summon the past for him to play with.
Thus, he is left to exercise his considerable, self-
begotten power, not in the antiseptic safety of a fantasy world, but in the evoked real world that becomes the target of his victimizing appetite. And
because he subsumes the objective world, subjects
it to his will, blind to his relation to the objective
world, he mistakes guilt (his responsibility for his
own acts) for innocence.

Freud describes the classic symptoms of the
narcissistic personality, of which megalomania is a
"secondary form," as an "over-estimation of the
power of wishes and mental processes, the 'omnipotence of thoughts,' a belief in the magical virtue

of words."[11] The clinical accuracy of the characters' narcissistic symptoms is striking. Jack and Howe share a belief in the magical power of words. Howe's "power was the arrangement and rearrangement of words . . . , a power great enough to control the world; but insane." Jack, however, comes to feel trapped by words. He projects a *"Self-Starting, Self-Stopping Word Machine"* in which he feels himself locked. The Word Machine, a metaphor for law, is a projection of Jack's superego with which he feels increasingly uncomfortable as his love for Elena grows. This discomfort is a sign of recuperation from the disease of narcissism. His confusion, his conflicting desires are a restorative where so many characters are driven by a single, compulsive vision.

Before he meets Elena, Jack contributes his time in order to defend civil rights cases in the South, but in doing so his deepest desire is not to insure justice for the single individual but to win the reins that control history. In describing the significance of civil rights victories, Jack says, "We made it happen . . . . That's the important thing, that we forced something into existence." Jack believed in "his own control, his own powerful will." He has the *hubris* of Hollingsworth in Hawthorne's *The Blithedale Romance* in whom the reformer's mask disguises the egotist: *"If I could locate the center of the universe . . . I'd have perfect leverage there to change everything."* But the healing fact is that he needs to mask his will to power under a reformer's cloak, that he feels guilt and is thus worthy of his later redemption by love.

Although Oates's world is essentially godless, there is in many of her novels something that the characters take for divinity, something that for them acts as the instrument of the absolute through which they envision their apotheosis. In *Do With Me What*

You Will both Marvin and Jack identify the law with the absolute. Marvin says, "We need the law because the law is what's left of divinity . . . . The law is holy. It will never be destroyed because there is no salvation outside it." If Marvin's assertions are sanctimonious, Jack's assertions are desperate: "All I have is a conviction . . . that the Law is permanent and will save us."

Marvin and Jack's equation of law with divinity is a particularly American equation, a deeply rooted symptom of our culture's attempt to sanctify itself. Oates has perhaps grasped an essential and underestimated fact of American culture: that law and lawyers are at its root. In a sense we are a country imagined, designed, and run by lawyers whose power, though secular, has remained unrivaled by other traditions or by religion. Most of the major figures of the American Revolution and Constitution were lawyers who saw their office as a priest does his. Bernard Bailyn records the obsessive concern expressed in revolutionary pamphlets that the Constitution "be grounded in some 'higher authority than the giving out temporary laws'."[12] But by the 1970's when Oates puts this idealism into the mouths of Marvin and Jack, the promise that these words originally carried has been perverted, and the faith of the lawyer, John Adams, which underlies this idealism, that "America was designed by Providence for the theatre on which man was to make his true figure" has proved delusionary.[13] In Oates's depiction of contemporary law, justice, guilt, and innocence have been subjected to a relativistic, godless universe and are thus rendered meaningless, except as words invoked to manipulate the emotions of a jury.

Just as words are wrenched from their meaning, criminals are wrenched from their crimes: Howe,

speaking to Ardis, says, "The law has nothing to do
with history, it doesn't replay history and make it
permanent, it doesn't provide us with scientific sen-
sory proof of anything . . . . It finds for the defendent
or for the prosecution . . . . There are no guilty people. The law establishes their guilt . . . . As for murderers . . . what do you mean by murderers?" Further, Jack says, "It was impossible, within the law,
not to achieve justice: if someone lost, someone else
won." Oates has made these lawyers the spokesmen
for relativity and for the Uncertainty Principle.
Howe's argument that there can be no irrefutable
knowledge of criminal acts is an argument declaring
everyone innocent. The effect of his sophistry is the
unmanning of the criminal; the chain of crime and
responsibility severed from the criminal, the act severed from the actor. Every criminal act that comes
under these lawyers' scrutiny becomes part of their
domain, to be re-created into a history over which
they preside as the agents of Providence. Thus the
law becomes a substitute for history and lawyers
become substitutes for God. Indeed, the law that
Jack says "will save us" and that Marvin says is our
salvation is a law that denies the Fall of man. If
everyone is innocent, Adam has never suffered a
division from God, has never been cast from the
Garden of Eden, has never had to encounter the
divided world outside. The law as it is practiced by
Howe and Jack shelters the undivided self by denying the reality outside the self.

Although the law is the way through which they
attempt to conquer and incorporate the immutable,
it is in the end dissatisfying. In a scene which demonstrates Oates's mastery of the grotesque, Howe
realizes it will not give him immortality. He invokes
the memory of an unusual bachelor party as an
image of all that Elena saves him from. The enter-

tainment includes women cyclists who, in the tradition of such events, are heavily made up and wear "feathers and sequins and all the usual junk." But what distinguishes these women is that they are very old; their faces are "masses of wrinkles." As Howe watches one of these women lose her balance and fall off of her bicycle, he feels "as if the bottom had dropped out of the universe," and he confronts the fact that he is "going to die."

This scene, like the one in which Shar (*With Shuddering Fall*) observes limbless people racing one another at a carnival side show, is a grotesque reminder of human limitation and of mortality. It is a powerful instance of Oates's deflationary art. Additionally, Jack discovers that his skill in the courtroom allows him to free the guilty but not the truly innocent. He is powerless to win a verdict of innocent for Mered Dawe, the only truly innocent man he has ever defended. As a result, his self-enclosed world crumbles, and he becomes vulnerable to love. Oates's art, in the best artistic tradition, is moral, intent on evoking exhortatory images. In her remarks on Sylvia Plath, we may glean the wider purpose of her megalomaniacs and narcissists: "I cannot emphasize strongly enough how valuable the experience of reading Plath can be, for it is a kind of 'dreaming back', a cathartic experience that not only cleanses us of our personal and cultural desires for regression, but explains by ways of its deadly accuracy what was wrong with such desires."[14]

As Ardis, Howe, and Morrissey are driven by the will to overcome, Elena is driven by the will to oblivion, an alternate form of the will to overcome; to Oates, both paths are paths of evasion. Her extreme passivity and vulnerability make her a spiritual sister of Maureen Wendall, of whom she is a

more beautiful version. Elena betrays a personality
that is in accord with Freud's description of the narcissistic female who is usually beautiful, but who
secludes herself within her beauty, impenetrable
to the outer world.[15] Because she is so beautiful, she
is able to live behind her face, to give her face to
the world instead of herself. It is her way of avoiding
the dangers of participation. Although Elena is a
sympathetic character throughout the novel, before
she acts she is indeed, as Ardis rightly describes
her, a "closed up narcissus."

Her character may have been partially inspired
by Oates's study of D. H. Lawrence's poetry (published separately by Black Sparrow Press in the
same year as the novel).[16] There is a particularly
interesting correspondence between Lawrence's
poem, "Blank," from which Oates quotes in her
essay, and the characterization of Elena. The passage below is the one she cites in her study:

> At present I am a blank, and I admit it.
> . . . So I am just going to go on being a blank,
>   till something nudges me from within
> and makes me know I am not blank any longer.

Elena is often referred to as "blank," she seeks
"invisibility" until "something nudges" her, love
and the acceptance of guilt, into consciousness.

With Elena, Oates is striking at Platonic idealism, at the Western notion of perfection. Significantly, Elena is a model, and before she acts, she
is described as enveloped in a vacuum, the still,
peaceful center of a world in motion. Her beauty
has an angelic quality; her hair "seemed to glow
about her head." Howe worships her because she
is "untouched," "outside of everything that's physical and degrading," "outside of the entire world."
The first time they meet, Jack is "bewildered" by

her "complete isolation," by "the neutrality of her being"; she is protected by an "invisible bell jar."[17] Ardis compares her perfection to the *"statues made of stone,"* which are outside of time. Elena is *"at the center, where everything is at peace."* Conscious that others see in her face an image of perfection identify her with that ideal, angelic image, Elena sometimes fears it will disappear and with it herself. She repeatedly checks her face in mirrors. Sitting in the night club where her mother works, "Elena could see herself faintly . . . in a frosted mirror not far away . . . the head of blond hair like a wire cloud around her head. She checked the image every few minutes to make sure it was still there." Before escaping with Jack, she consistently objectifies her mirror image—*"There is Elena Howe in the mirror"*—never feeling at one with it.[18]

In the eyes of others, Elena's beauty has put her beyond reality, at the transcendent "still center" of the revolving world toward which the pilgrim in T. S. Eliot's poetry strives. Indeed Elena's movement through the novel is an inversion of the movement of Eliot's pilgrim. Characteristically, just as Eliot's pilgrim gropes toward perfect wholeness, Oates's heroine gropes toward division, imperfection. As Ardis and Howe negotiate the marriage contract, Elena fantasizes dyeing her hair black in order to "stain every hair, every single thin miraculous blond hair, every part of her scalp, her soul . . . ." Only in love, in the division of consciousness into self and other does she achieve a redeeming completion. Only in Jack's gaze, does she finally see a "perfect reflection" of herself "as in a mirror." Opposed to Narcissus, who is completed in his own image, Elena finds completion only when the self overflows into the other.

As in *Wonderland,* Oates underpins the novel

with womb and pregnancy imagery. In contrast to
Wonderland, however, this imagery does not signify
insularity, but a yielding of the narcissistic ego to
something beyond the self. Shelley views her womb
as barren; Helen resents the process of pregnancy
that intrudes on her singleness; but for Elena, the
womb and pregnancy become symbols of her liberation from self-enclosure. Indeed, Oates describes the gathering of Elena's final courage with
this imagery. In a passage in which Elena recalls
a cocktail-party conversation, she wistfully remem-
bers that *"that day I learned from them about the
immortality of the womb: you can't kill it."* Re-
belling against her husband's prohibition against
children and against her mother's warning, *"You
don't want children . . . . Don't ruin yourself,"* she
says, *"And now I want a child. And I want that
child to carry me in his head forever . . . ."* Part I
ends with Elena mesmerized by the Alger Memorial
statue of a gigantic man holding the sun in one hand
and a man, a woman, and an infant in the other. At
first puzzled by the statue, she reads the inscription:
" *'God, through the Spirit of Man, is manifested in
the family, the noblest human relationship . . .'* "
and thinks, *"Yes, I understand what is being said."*
She feels her lover "embedded in her womb"; Oates
describes Elena's love for Jack as a "pregnancy."
Elena compares her need for Jack to *"a kick inside
me; the kick of an embryo."* The form of Elena's
defiance is a decision to escape Marvin's protective,
narcissistic, barren Eden in order to enter fully into
the life process, to submit to the division of self that
the images of wombs and pregnancy and the symbol
of the Alger Memorial suggest.

While Elena accepts herself as an ideal object,
she is subjectively invisible. Struck by the "vivid
not thereness of her face," Elena thinks it ironic that

her "perfect beauty" is a "substitute for existence."
In a crucial speech, Howe states, "Things move
from invisibility to visibility." When "the terrible
ghosts inside us . . . rush out into the world . . . a
'crime' is committed" and we become visible. Thus
when Elena commits crimes, when she abandons
Marvin, despite his claim that his salvation depends
on her love, and she abducts Jack from an ordinary,
"invisible" marriage and his adopted child, she becomes "visible"; she enters history and time. Oates
describes Elena's victory as a victory of crime, of
evil, of adulthood: "Never in her life had she conquered any territory, achieved any victories. Never.
Never had she been selfish, never evil or adult. And
now if she wanted Morrissey she would cross over
into adulthood to get him, into the excitement of
evil." If in *Wonderland* we witness the spasms of
the American Faust as he sees his imperial ideal
fade in the exigencies of living, in *Do With Me What
You Will* we witness the American Adam and Eve
eat of the apple, as the law—the contemporary form
of divinity—jealously watches.[19] Freud reported
that the narcissistic personality often effects a self-
cure by falling in love, and although Freud complained that this "cure by love" is not as effective
as the "cure by analysis," in the realm of art, it is
infinitely more satisfying.[20]

Yet Oates is reluctant to endorse this "cure by
love" as a final cure, and her reluctance is embodied
in the mystic, Mered Dawe. With Dawe, Oates in-
serts another plane of consciousness into the novel,
one that has the effect of mitigating Elena's victory,
emphasizing the pathos with which her victory is
imbued. Ironically, Mered is the only innocent person to go to trial in this novel and the only person
who is convicted, after an ineffectual, though sincere defense by Jack.[21] A prophet in the Oriental

mode, he preaches a "non-mechanical reality," in
which true reality exists as "mind-stuff," "light-
love." Elena, who operates as an indicator of where
our sympathies should lie, calls him her "truest
lover." She tells him to "dream me." However, in
the series of letters he sends from the prison hospital
to the judge who presided over his trial is traced
Mered's progressive psychosis that takes the form
of an obsessive fear of impotence and that ends with
his final submission to the judgment of the court.

In his first letters, he argues his innocence with
facts, real evidence. In a subsequent letter, he uses
Marvin's argument that "it is not demonstrable by
any known scientific method that certain deeds
have or have not occurred, since all . . . alleged vi-
olators . . . have evolved since the historical time at
which the 'crime' allegedly took place . . . ." In his
relenting, last letter he writes, "I hope [I] will be
someday totally fulfilled in your judgment and an-
nihilated in my own profane being." In other words,
he enters a plea of *nolo contendere*—do with me
what you will—the only such plea entered in this
novel.[22] Thus the only alternative to admitting guilt,
to accepting the fallen stature of man, is an annihi-
lation of selfhood, a total mystical submission, a
transcendent impotence; but it is a pathological alternative, not viable in what we know as the sane
world. Yet Oates's juxtaposition of Mered's spiritual
victory with the lovers' profane victory results in a
final vision that is complex and ambivalent, a vision
violently resisting comfortable, nostalgic answers,
a vision that is in continual process.

8

Toward Pluralism:

The Assassins:

A Book of Hours

Although the consciousness of Mered Dawe provides a glimpse of another world that at the same
time seems to diminish or put into ironic perspective the victory of love over law, it is not uncondi-
tionally the higher, the sovereign, consciousness
because, as indicated in the previous chapter, Oates
hints that what appears as vision may also be pathology. In *Do With Me What You Will*, Oates entertains the possibility of a higher consciousness,
but she regards it with skepticism. That Mered represents simply another, not necessarily better, plane
of consciousness becomes clearer in the light of
Oates's next two novels, *The Assassins: A Book of
Hours* and *Childwold*, which are from a very general view explorations of the isolation and clash of
very different consciousnesses. Oates is as sympathetic to Dawe as was William James to the "twice-
born," people who have experienced conversion
dreams, whose testimonies appear in his *The Varieties of Religious Experience*, and like James, she
is unwilling to relinquish the multifold, experiential
world to *any* single, incorporating vision.[1]

As becomes evident in *The Assassins (1975)*,
Oates offers her most sympathetic characters as
martyrs and saints to a Jamesian, pluralistic universe

and for final visions, she substitutes the vision of an indeterminate universe. It is a vision of a world without a center, a mysterious, terrifying world but one that contains enough lines of continuity, if one will recognize them, to form a net which provides the individual with a sustaining context for his life, though not with absolute safety. A pluralistic, undetermined universe, as William James saw, is always open to the assaults of "chance," to the unpredictable, and against these assaults, the individual is "impotent," although to submit wholly to impotence is as deathly as to fantasize omnipotence.[2] Hugh in *The Assassins* declares: "Alas, a devilish fine line between omnipotence and impotence."

The Assassins is a complex experiment in form and theme. In it, Oates has relinquished the third-person narrative and a controlling, central consciousness for the stream of consciousness form of the interior monologue. In fact, in this novel, form becomes theme, for Oates creates characters who are locked within their own egos, within their isolated stream of consciousness, fated to spin monologues, never able to enter into the reciprocity of dialogue. There are three such monologues belonging to Hugh, Yvonne, and Stephen Petrie, respectively. The fictional occasion for the story is the death (which is presumed to be an assassination) of Andrew Petrie, a onetime United States senator and famous political theorist, the most successful of the contemporary Petrie clan. Like Faulkner's *The Sound and the Fury*, the same story is told from different—in this case three—points of view. It is the darkest of all of Oates's novels in that no character achieves initiation, or even manages to penetrate beyond the confines of his ego, although Stephen, a religious mystic and the most sympathetic of the three characters, does survive.

The novel's subtitle, *A Book of Hours*, refers to the canonical book of hours that traditionally ends with the Office of the Dead. When questioned about the choice of subtitle, Oates gave the somewhat sly explanation that the novel is a meditation on death.[3] Despite the fact that the plot and characters converge on Andrew's death, that Hugh's section is replete with death imagery, and that Yvonne's section is woven with images of the truncation of the life-process (miscarriage, abortion), the book is more a meditation on cultural and psychological death than physical death.

Oates carefully traces the Petrie lineage to its Puritan roots. Andrew writes that the Puritans were deluded because *"they thought it was God directing them, but in fact it was history."* In depicting the Petrie clan through the centuries, Oates makes it clear that the disease of the imperial self from which the contemporary Petries suffer, has its origins in the first American Petrie. Hugh describes his ancestor as "a deranged Puritan minister—famous for the transactions viciousness can make with civilization." Just as in Faulkner, where the Snopes's new South is in some ways the natural heir of the Compson's old South, so the imperial self is an evolution of the Puritan vision. The Puritans' notions of divine "election" and divine "errand," the delusion that *they* were God's chosen, sent by Him to build the New Jerusalem in America, finds its modern analogue in the secular zeal for power and wealth.[4] Subsequent Petries were governors, senators, presidential advisers, wealthy landowners, and industrialists, accumulating God's grace in tangible pieces.[5]

In fact, the regular appearance of God to the various members of the Petrie tribe through the centuries conveniently follows on the heels of their fi-

nancial, political, or other worldly failure. The Petries find God (except for Stephen, who is genuine)
when they lose the world. An eighteenth-century
Petrie, Aaron, "heard the voice of God" when he
had retired from politics after ordering the senseless
massacre of some factory workers. The father of
Andrew, Hugh, and Stephen, a cruel, grasping, sadistic man who drove his wife to suicide, also finds
God—in the midst of a heart attack:

Nearly dying and being rescued—resuscitated—raised
from the dead by Our Lord—in the form of a machine—
His presence revealed to me as a white, glowing, throbbing, palpitating, *living* machine—surrounded by agents,
mere men, mortals, men and women in white—agents of
God—wired to do His bidding . . . .

The passage is an admirable example of black
humor, but more important, it is an emblem of the
staggering, narcissistic arrogance inherent in all
Petrie endeavors. Whether they endeavor to accumulate power, or wealth, or divinity—or to survive
a heart attack—they feel themselves to be divinely
sanctioned. A Petrie is ever convinced that he is
"elected," whether by God or by history. The Puritan confidence in divine purpose turns in modern,
relativistic times to the confidence that particular
individuals have in their own discrete, absolute visions, as Oates exemplifies in her portrayal of Stephen, Hugh, and Andrew. Thus the Puritan obsession with "election" is the historical justification
for latter-day overreaching and incorporation. The
parallels between the Petries and American myth
and aspirations *are* obvious; from America as New
Jerusalem to America as superpower is merely a lex-
ical leap.

Oates's meditation results in a deeply pessimistic book, the terms of which offer no redeeming

possibilities. As one strain in the book argues that the predilection for incorporating visions is the culture's historical inheritance, a complementary strain argues that the individual's fate may be sealed by this inheritance. Perhaps the most pessimistic idea on which Oates meditates is that character is fate. Hugh declares, "my character is my fate—*his* [Andrew] character was *his* fate, inescapable. We experience nothing but what we already are." The concept, from the Stoics, is summarized by F. H. Sandbach: "In the last analysis a man's character is formed not by any choice between open alternatives, but by his environment and the impression made on him by the external world. These are all due to Fate, which therefore determines what he is."[6] The individual's personality as formed by his culture circumscribes the limits of his existence and determines the path he will take to his death. Despite Oates's emphasis, especially in the early novels, on fate, on the circumstances into which one is born, *The Assassins* explores the darker side of this idea; the novel is a study of, a meditation on, this kind of death—the complete isolation of the individual in his personality.

In *A Garden of Earthly Delights, them,* and *Wonderland,* the protagonists spend their time attempting to recover from catastrophic events by secluding themselves in narcissistic fantasies. The destructive agent is external, cultural, coming in the form of the Depression and race riots. Although the characters of *Do With Me What You Will* are also subjected to extreme experiences—Elena's abduction and Jack's father's murder trial—these experiences do not come directly out of the culture, but result from the rages of sick minds. The culture appears as a formative rather than a cataclysmic or antagonistic force. The impetus for the plot is not an external event so much as the personalities of the characters themselves. Oates seems to be shifting the emphasis from external agency to internal agency (though the internal is always a manifestation of larger cultural tendencies). This shift has prompted her experimentation with the stream of consciousness form in *The Assassins* and *Childwold*. Moreover, this formal experimentation coincides with a broader, more definitive, philosophical articulation of her vision of reality. In an Oates novel, survival depends upon the ability to become initiated, and the refusal to be initiated results in destruction. In *The Assassins*, it becomes clear that what initiates conform to, and what noninitiates violate, is the very nature of reality that Oates, following William James, regards as pluralistic.[7]

Many aspects of the novel suggest William James. In fact, the Petrie family history somewhat resembles the Jameses'. The first American Petrie was an English emigrant, a Puritan minister who established the Petrie wealth; the first American James, William, was an Irish emigrant and strict Calvinist who built the Jameses' wealth. Albany, where the emigrant William James dies and where Henry James Sr. was born is the home of the Petries. Both families reached their peak in the nineteenth-century. Like Henry James Sr., Stephen Petrie, as well as some of his ancestors, experiences a conversion dream. Oates invents a specific connection between the Jameses and the Petries in that she makes Susan Petrie Montague one of the partners of the Irish emigrant William James (William James's grandfather who outlived three wives).[8] Moreover, the "stream of consciousness" style of the novel also suggests William James in that James popularized this metaphor for the process of consciousness.[9] In her recent short story volume, *Night-Side*, the stories "Night-Side" and "A Theory of Knowledge" take place in the late nineteenth-century and concern characters who resemble figures in the James circle. In addition, there are specific references to and echoes of William James's writings.

Perhaps more important, the underlying *Weltanschauung* of the novel is William Jamesian. Its underpinning of Jamesian pluralism is symbolized in the controlling images of the river and the multibranched willow tree on the abandoned Petrie farm where Andre Petrie dies and where Yvonne has a horrible dream-fantasy, in which she imagines herself shot and hacked to pieces.

The fact that each of the characters is dominated by a single vision, with which he attempts to explain and control reality, suggests James's "monism," reality as ordered from a single, absolute point of view, a philosophical stance that James spent his lifetime attempting to invalidate and against which he posited pluralism:

Pragmatically interpreted, pluralism or the doctrine that it is many means only that the sundry parts of reality *may be externally related*. Everything you can think of, however vast or inclusive, has on the pluralistic view a genuinely 'external' environment of some sort or amount. Things are 'with' one another in many ways, but nothing includes everything, or dominates over everything . . . . Pluralism lets things really exist in the each-form or distributively. Monism thinks that all the all-form or collective-unit form is the only form that is rational.[10]

Although Oates translates James's concept of "monism" into her concept of the "isolated ego," her allegiance with James is clear. Oates echoes these Jamesian thoughts in her statement: "It is doubtful . . . that nature is really so mute, so unintelligent, as alienated personalities seem to think; it is certainly doubtful that the human ego, the 'I' is in any

significant way isolated from the vast, living totality
of which it is a part."[11]

The following passage from "A Pluralistic
Universe" reveals James's vehemence against the
monist or absolutist position: "The advocates of the
absolute assure us that any distributive form of
being is infected and undermined by self-contra-
diction. If we are unable to assimilate their argu-
ments, and we have been unable, the only course
we can take, it seems to me, is to let the absolute
bury the absolute, and to seek reality in more promising directions, even among the details of the finite
and the immediately given."[12] Oates modernizes
James's vocabulary, and for "monism" she substitutes the term, "gigantic paranoid-delusion system": "The stasis celebrated in much of contemporary literature, the erecting of gigantic paranoid-
delusion systems that are self-enclosed and self-de-
structing, argues for a simple failure of reasoning:
the human ego has too long imagined itself the supreme form of consciousness in the universe."[13]

James said that "compromise and mediation are
inseparable from the pluralistic philosophy. Only
monistic dogmatism can say of any of its hypotheses,
'It is either that or nothing; take it or leave it just
as it stands.' "[14] And it is just this that the "monistic
dogmatists" of Oates's *The Assassins* can and do say.
Their rigidity affords no room for compromise and
for Oates this rigidity is the death stance. The monism of Andrew and Yvonne consists of a belief in
the absolute power of reason to the exclusion of all
else. At one point Yvonne recalls that Andrew flirted
with the "radical empiricism" of "William James."
But he rejected it, finding it "too atomistic," a
"nightmare," *"like a sea of maggots on a carrion."*
The image of maggots is from James's "The Dilemma of Determinism"; the exact quotation reads,

"A friend . . . once told me that the thought of my universe made him sick, like the sight of the horrible motion of a mass of maggots in their carrion bed."[15] In order to counteract this Jamesian indeterminist "nightmare," Andrew builds a temple of reason, constructed of carefully chosen, logically ordered words within which he and Yvonne attempt, unsuccessfully, to dwell.

Andrew is a figure out of Oates's gallery of megalomaniacs, whose audacity perhaps outstrips other figures in this gallery. In middle age he resists the laurels of public office in order to work out a philosophy that would *"change our way of thinking . . . would change our lives . . ."* In preparation for what he feels is the inevitable atomic destruction of the world, he promotes a "Post-Apocalyptic" organization that would somehow rule by reason. Yvonne's recollection of Andrew's image immediately before his death is an articulation of the conflict energizing the novel: the conflict between the order the individual imposes on reality, an order that falsifies it, and reality itself that Oates sees as pluralistic.

He brought . . . a small clock in its leather traveling case, though he has a wristwatch; he props the clock up on the mantel where he can see it whenever he glances around. Time, time! . . . He likes to hear it clicking and whining and whirring, so that its terrible passage will not be too surprising. He brought a dictaphone too but he never uses it. And the papers: the mammoth collection of papers. Sharpened pencils, ballpoint pens in several colors of ink, fast-drying marker pens, an eraser, a pencil sharpener, and a yellow notepad and a stack of typewriter paper and a newly published dictionary, still in its glossy black jacket. Outside is the river, shallow and noisy, inside is a small quiet kingdom where the clock ticks peacefully and everything is being brought into order, brought into completion and perfection.

The juxtaposition of the river with Andrew's small kingdom in which he has amassed articles in preparation for a rite of the intellect is, of course, ironic, for no matter to what completion and perfection he brings his kingdom, his imperialism will never succeed in dominating the river.

All of the characters suffer from a different failure of vision. As Andrew and Yvonne reduce reality to intellect, Hugh, a caricaturist, reduces it to the two-dimensional, and Stephen reduces it to God. None has access to the meaning of the river and the "immense" willow tree that it nourishes. Andrew says of the tree:

I was amazed by its size and complexity . . . eight main trunks and they divide into twelve or thirteen small trunks, each large and sturdy enough to be, to have been, separate trees. It was colossal . . . astonishing . . . mysterious. One tree, or many? Many trees competing for moisture, or a single tree, nourished by a single source?

Though transformed into highly metaphoric language, this question echoes a passage from James's "What Pragmatism Means":

Is the world one or many?—fated or free?—material or spiritual?—here are notions either of which may or may not hold good of the world; and disputes over such notions are unending . . . . What difference would it practically make to anyone if this notion rather than that notion were true? If no practical difference whatever can be traced, then the alternatives mean practically the same thing, and all dispute is idle . . . . That is, the rival views mean practically the same thing, and meaning, other than practical there is for us none.[16]

The sense James evokes in his philosophy is of the impenetrability of the mystery of the universe; in Oates, to attempt to penetrate it is to assure self-defeat. Yet it is just this mystery that the characters in *The Assassins* cannot accept, a refusal that destroys them. Andrew writes, "Clarity is close to godliness; and when you achieve clarity, you can dispense with godliness."

The specific mystery that consumes the characters is who assassinated Andrew Petrie? The degree to which the characters are obsessed by it is evident from a letter Hugh writes to Yvonne shortly before his suicide attempt: "How can we live? How? Without knowing? How can we bear it not knowing? How and why and in what context he died . . . . It isn't a question of justice, dear Yvonne, but of the survival of sanity; mankind cannot live with mystery . . . . At least I can't." In the course of the novel we discover that Andrew probably committed suicide although Oates never makes this clear, thus playfully pointing to her reader's hunger for solutions.

It is perhaps Oates's ironic achievement that some of her reviewers called this novel a "whodunit" because "whodunit," the solution to the mystery, is something always withheld, not only withheld but irrelevant.[17] It never occurs to Andrew's relatives that he committed suicide, which is indicative of their inability to formulate the correct question, let alone discover the answer. They are so intent on discovering an assassin, so obsessed with the mystery, that each entertains the possibility—contradictory to fact—of his own guilt. The mystery of the novel implies the larger mystery of Truth and the individual's incapacity to approach it. Towards the end of her section of the novel Yvonne achieves a fleeting, epiphanal glance at the symbolic import of the river: "Everything ends at the river . . . everything yearns for that place and for the ceaseless noise of the water, part music, part inaudible conversation, part chaotic din." This is an image of the encompassing mystery of life that renders all quests for Truth irrelevant.

Although Jamesian pluralism provides the novel with a positive framework against which the characters' monisms may be judged, in the body of the novel Oates dramatizes the psychological implications of Einstein's theory of relativity. Einsteinian physics proposes that physical laws are dependent on the frame of reference from which they are described, that physical properties are not absolute, but dependent upon the system used to describe them.[18] If each character may be said to be a "system," a frame of reference, a point of view from which reality is ordered, then the novel is an investigation of the fact that, to paraphrase Yvonne, people's realities do not coincide. Not only do the characters' metaphysics conflict, but they do not even share an objective reality.[19]

Although Stephen, Hugh and Andrew are brothers, their versions of their childhood differ radically. For Hugh, childhood was a series of humiliations; for Stephen it was a series of encounters with God; for Andrew it was a series of victories. Even when they share a particular experience, the objective facts elude them. For instance, Hugh and Andrew have disparate recollections of their childhood prank of climbing on the roof of their house. Hugh recalls that Andrew enticed him upon the roof with taunts of cowardice. His memory is characteristically bitter, blaming Andrew for the foolish adventure, for his paralysis with fear, for the humiliation of having to admit his fear. Andrew's memory of the incident, on the other hand, is dominated by the fact that he fell off the roof, resulting in a snapped thighbone and a crushed kneecap. This is a fact Hugh does not recall.

Similar incidents are prevalent throughout the book: Andrew's funeral is experienced differently by all three characters; encounters the characters have with each other are reshaped according to the personality relating them; even minor data are colored by the individual perceiver. Hugh and Yvonne, for instance, have antithetical perceptions of Yvonne's ring. Hugh, an impotent homosexual, haunted by recurrent nightmares of an Amazonian woman with exaggerated and threatening sexual characteristics, describes the ring as a "platinum or white gold ring" with "snakes dancing on their tails, woven together." To Yvonne, for whom intellect is the supreme reality, the ring appears made of "inexpensive silver, two half-moons facing each other." The ring reflects the image of the perceiver; in the Einsteinian world, reality is a mirror. To Hugh it appears an erotic taunt, while to Yvonne it is an appropriately colder image. Thus their preception of an already elusive reality is further distorted by the monisms that possess them.

It nevers occurs to Oates's "monistic dogmatists" that reality has no discernable order. Hugh says, "The difficulty with stories, even true ones, is that they begin nowhere and end nowhere. Ultimately they encompass the entire universe and all of history. Yet—one must begin somewhere, after all! order must be imposed upon events! *History* must be presented as a story!" Although there is an element of the artist's self-mockery in this aphoristic statement, its central perception is that order is an imposition on, rather than an inherent property of, reality. Moreover, it is a subjective order and therefore one that isolates rather than illuminates, bringing despair. Hugh declares, "The adults of the world? All, all in disguise." To Yvonne "the world was composed of strangers." The final Stephen, defeated and guilt-ridden, sounds the pessimistic note that "everyone was doomed."

Oates's characters are destroyed by their adherence to a monist view of the world that alienates them not from an objective reality, which according to Einsteinian physics is not accessible to absolute definition, but from a shared reality and from each other. The tenacity with which Oates has these characters cling to their compulsive design of reality is an artistic exaggeration that points to all of us, even, as the aphorism about the fictional process suggests, to herself as an artist. What prevails, finally, is mystery, and against that the monists' visions—Hugh's of the world reduced to the "I," Yvonne's of the world reduced to reason, Stephen's of the world reduced to God—are impotent. Realities not only do not, but cannot, coincide because the very concept of "*a* reality," of a single point of view ordering the world, is a falsification of it.

Although each of the characters is trapped within the confines of his own personality, there is a movement in the novel, a regressive movement in fact, which begins with Hugh's stream of consciousness. He is completely paralyzed: blind, deaf, mute, and sustained by an iron lung. His first sentence reads, "I was born." The last sentence of the novel closes Stephen's section, and it reads, "I can accommodate myself to anything." Thus the novel begins with the narcissistic "I" and ends with total accommodation. It moves from the reduction of reality to the "I"—Hugh's reality is literally limited to the contents of his own mind—to a suspension of the effort to engage reality. Moreover, each consciousness that we encounter is a resonance of an historical period, ordered so that we are, so to speak, drawn backwards in time, though the actual time span of the novel is one year—from the spring of Andrew's death to the following spring. Hugh's paralysis, his obsession with death, the whole tenor of his section suggests that he is a portrait of the pessimistic strains in the contemporary consciousness. Yvonne's philosophy that "ideas are the only reality," her infatuation with the mind and reason, and the fact that her section is littered with the names of philosophers suggest that she represents that strain in the postmedieval, precontemporary consciousness that relied on the intellect for explanations of the universe. Stephen, God-obsessed, represents the medieval consciousness. (All three, of course, also represent strains in contemporary culture.) In light of Oates's belief that during the Renaissance, man's attention shifted from God to the "I," it is significant that Hugh and Yvonne are destroyed while Stephen, the only pre-Renaissance consciousness, survives. He, like the medieval society of which he is a latter-day representative, endures the loss of God; but rather than follow the historical precedent of substituting the "I" for "God," he chooses the path of nonattachment, homelessness. The fact that this circumstance leaves him as the only character whose fate is not "fixed" is suggestive as well. Although for the Buddhists, homelessness is a prerequisite to Nirvana, for Western man it is an evasion; but by pointing to Stephen, who has managed to break out of his monism, Oates is also pointing to an alternative to the "I"-centered existence, an alternative to the path on which the Renaissance placed us.

Hugh is not an artist as he claims but a caricaturist, and it is the reductive philosophy of caricature and its specific application in Hugh's work that helps to articulate the larger context of this section of the novel.[20] Hugh tells us that like the foun-

der of his art, "Annibale Carracci of Bologna," his
ideal is *to grasp the perfect deformity, and thus
reveal the very essence of a personality."* Further,
Hugh, perhaps the most self-obsessed of Oates's
narcissists, states his aim as: "The triumph of Hugh
Petrie over . . . everyone . . . . To reduce a man to
one or two traits, to twist them into the features of
animals—to flatten the complex deceiving contours
of the face to two dimensions . . . . Far more effective than actual murder." This reductionism is the
narcissist's triumph not only over the rest of humanity but over the whole of civilization: "We're
tired of being civilized . . . . Tired of being three
dimensions—The Great Men and Women of our
Era: freaky line drawings."

For Oates the reduction of the world to the
isolated ego is a form of death, and she illustrates
this belief in her portrayal of Hugh by connecting
the reductionism of his art to an exaltation of death.
Hugh's drawings, his fantasies, and his conscious
life are dominated by the image of death. Oates
weaves a motif of funerals through his section;
nearly every time that Hugh looks out of his Greenwich Village apartment, he observes a funeral taking
place at the funeral parlor across the street. He considers as a work of genius his drawing of a "copu-
lation-crucifixion" in which the Angel of Death is
crucified on the image of a woman drawn upside
down. His Christ is Death and the cross that he
bears is not sin, but the life-generating force as symbolized by the woman. His is that artistic vision
obsessed with the idea of man under sentence of
death. He has replaced the worship of God with the
worship of Death: "The Angel of Death had guided
everything—had always been in control." His vision reflects the pessimism of so much of modern
art, a pessimism drived from the philosophy of Scho-

penhauer, in which death is the central, controlling fact of life and thus all else is meaningless. But by putting this vision in the mouth of a greedy, impotent, alcoholic, homosexual, hypochondriac caricaturist, Oates does much to diminish its credibility.

The opening passages of Hugh's section are cryptic and ominous because Oates does not reveal until the end of the section that he is paralyzed and that we have been listening to the thoughts of a man who is literally locked in his consciousness. He is forty and the middle of the three brothers; he has won some small fame (so he claims) with his book *Eminent Contemporaries* that includes a caricature of his brother Andrew. He is bitterly jealous of his elder brother's enormous successes which are a measure of his own failure. (Before Andrew's death, he fantasizes hiring assassins to murder him or assassinating Andrew himself). His obsession with his brother's assassination and with his brother's widow, who he is convinced can illuminate the mystery of his death, causes a rapid deterioration in an already neurasthenic personality. Appropriately, he is plagued by extreme near-sightedness and a progressively aggravating ear infection. His physical and psychological ailments intensify as his obsession with Andrew's death grows. Dissatisfied with the reductive analysis his Freudian psychoanalyst, Dr. Wynand offers, Hugh consults a Jungian analyst, Dr. Swann.

In Dr. Swann's analysis we hear Oates speaking, and James as well: "The art of which you speak . . . is an infant's revenge upon the adults who surround him . . . . Your 'art'—your caricatures—what value have they?—what hold have they given you in the world? Vanity—foppery—cruelty—a tragic delusion you share with your era . . . . Certain

visions are forbidden us . . . . If your distinguished
brother was murdered—what is that to you, to the
burden of your own life? You must let him go . . . .
You must live with your impotence." Hugh violently opposes Swann's universe of mystery and impotence, a universe that he cannot overcome, preferring Wynand's simplistic reductions, which locate
all neurosis in Oedipal rage. He answers Swann
with a battery of epithets, word-cartoons, the reply
with which his reductive art always meets truth:
"Dwarf ! Monkey! *Walking Corpse!*" [Italics mine].

Hugh's life, like his art, inevitably falls into
farce, into caricature. He says, "Around the hero, it
is said, everything turns to tragedy. And around
Hugh Petrie? Comedy, cruel hissing laughter."
Hugh tells us that as a college student his cousin
Pamela, in collusion with Andrew, enticed him into
a sexual encounter. When he could not perform,
they ridiculed him, the episode designed for this
end. Humiliated, he plans to commit suicide, but
at the crucial moment, he is interrupted by a "sneez-
ing fit!" His second, more successful attempt is executed at a posh restaurant, but when the moment
approaches the tragic, he cannot resist playing the
clown instead of the would-be martyr. He draws the
attention of the lunch crowd by using his ventrilo-
quism to throw his voice to the fish on his plate who
begins to protest his "position." Hugh then "shoots
his impudent brook trout" with a pistol stolen from
Andrew's first wife and "without flinching," places
the barrel in his own mouth, but thinking of Wynand, puts it to his forehead instead. This clever
switch defeats his purpose—he succeeds in transforming himself not into the martyr demonstrating
the stupidity of the age as he had hoped but into a
permanent paralytic. He suffers the fate to which
his character and his particular monist vision have

contracted him: he becomes a physical caricature of himself. Indeed, the scene provides compelling evidence of Oates's mastery of black humor.

In fact, there is much in Hugh's characterization to suggest that Oates is parodying the black comedy of Samuel Beckett, who works in the tradition of man under the sentence of death. Oates has spoken of Beckett as "almost inaccessible to us . . . whose monologue novels are an expression of a particular self, almost selfless, pared to an existence devoid of the 'world' as we know it."[21] Hugh's paralysis suggests those reknowned Beckett characters who are distinguished by their physical paralysis that in Beckett's vision symbolize the human condition. Like many of Beckett's characters, Hugh is adept at vaudeville. He is clownish, an amateur magician, and a ventriloquist. His frequent encounters with tramps and panhandlers suggest Beckett's tramps. However, Oates reverses Beckett's assumptions; in her parody, the paralysis is a result of the individual's act, not the *a priori* condition of life. It is the appropriate fate of a deluded, farcical nature. As opposed to Beckett, in whose works paralysis and farce are elevated to high tragedy, the potentially tragic in Hugh's life inevitably reverts to farce, the deserved punishment for what is to Oates a pathetic failure of vision.

Oates contrasts Hugh's exaltation of the grotesque, misanthropic cartoons that flow from his pen, cartoons burdened with figures who are "clawing squirming biting wrestling disembowelling one another," with his horror of the ordinary look of humanity. "One of the ugliest visions of my life," says Hugh, is of

a woman on the curb watching intently as our funeral procession passed . . . . In her forties, probably. Wearing

tight red shorts and a pullover blouse . . . a woman not
really fat, not freakish, not insane—just a woman, a shop-
per, quite normal for the era . . . . It was the era watching
us, the era itself—the normality of it—standing there on
the curb, inexplicably disgusting to me, infinitely mysterious, as alien to me as if she belonged to another species altogether.

The woman in red shorts is Oates's image of a humanity antithetical to her rapacious narcissists and
megalomaniacs. She could be the full-bodied, life-
embracing Arlene of *Childwold* or Loretta of *them*,
figures for whom the universe need not be understood or overcome. The universe does not loom before them as a mystery to be solved; they accept the
indeterminate world they find themselves in and
with small efforts explore its possibilities, submit
to its processes. Thus they feel regret but not doom,
failure but not despair. Not only does Oates contrast
the normality of the woman in red shorts with Hugh
but with Yvonne as well. From the woman in red
shorts, Hugh's glance turns to Yvonne: "Mournful,
leaden-pale . . . . She was pure, and the other woman
was defiled." The adjectives he employs all suggest
lifelessness, and within this scheme, defilement is
preferable to purity.

Yvonne, born of working class parents, meets
Andrew in her mid-twenties. He is already divorced
from his first wife, and after a short courtship, they
marry. Her personal history consists of a series of
rejections of emotional relationships that would en-
mesh her with another in undefinable ways. She
prefers the more predictable relationships of the
mind. For instance, she feels that her "primary connection" to Andrew is "through the mind, through
the antagonism of their minds." After Andrew's
death, Yvonne carries on his work, editing and com-
pleting his manuscripts, presenting his ideas at con-

ferences, and overseeing the publication of his journal, *Discourses*.[22]

Oates depicts Yvonne as so utterly secluded in the life of the intellect that she appears "dead," a "statue," and she reminds Hugh of a mannequin in a Saks department store window. Oates also describes her as "horsey," "coltish," thus suggesting Swift's Houyhnhnms in *Gulliver's Travels*, creatures of reason who deny their brute physicality and with whom Swift satirized the rationalists of his time. Yvonne "felt an unaccountable satisfaction" in her twenty-sixth floor apartment, "a kind of tower, quite safe." Oates imbues her with the appropriate psychological disease of paranoia that Yvonne herself describes as "the inability to tolerate ambiguity," a disease whereby the mind creates an impeccable, internally logical edifice of cause and effect within whose chambers it dwells oblivious to reality outside. Yvonne sees "enemies" everywhere; everyone she meets is regarded as potentially dangerous.

As Hugh suffers from impotence, Yvonne suffers from frigidity. To her, sex requires endurance, not participation. Of the four sexual encounters described, none results in orgasm for either partner. After drugging her in order to rape her, Hugh in typically farcical fashion cannot overcome his impotence to execute his plan. Wunsch, a teacher of the mentally handicapped, suffers the same debility with Yvonne. Eliot, the new editor of *Discourses*, is too drunk. Harvey, Andrew's cousin, after an agonizing and labored attempt, withdraws without achieving climax.

Through Yvonne, Oates meditates on the fantasy that the intellect can bring man to a final understanding. Yvonne's compulsion is to discover "a reason for everything. Nothing without its reasons. Causality: sanity. Chaos: insanity." Yvonne worships "the intellect and its precise measurements, its setting up of empires . . . ." Her physical ailments—Yvonne suffers from fainting spells and irregularities in her menstrual cycle—are the body's reassertive rages against the mind. The image that haunts her is of maggots, an image Oates derived from a previously quoted James passage, a negative image of pluralism, and of the seething, squirming, physical life that so repulses Yvonne.

Oates suggests that the overestimation of intellect is a way of objectifying existence. Before Yvonne's disillusionment with Andrew's work, she sees herself as an instrument of circumstance: "There was Andrew, there was his work. There was the fact of her widowhood. The circumstances were incontestable; her own existence, so problematic, was not an issue." Yet when disillusionment finally comes, she does not allow "her own existence" to surface. After she orders his papers and disclaims her interest in them, she "aborts" his "shadow": "It had filled her womb for a while . . . . It had clamped itself inside her, wanting to eat her alive, but she had expelled it . . . ." She drives to the abandoned Petrie farm, the scene of Andrew's death. It is spring, nearly the anniversary of her husband's death, and at the bank of the "swollen and noisy" river, near the willow tree, the woman of intellect fantasizes a horrible, primitive, ritualistic death, a blood-sacrifice to the river of life and the tree of mystery, which claim her despite her resistance.

Although Oates derides the contemporary obsession with death in her characterization of Hugh and the obsession with intellect in her characterization of Yvonne, she is ready to sympathize with Stephen whose obsession is with God, though she maintains a long, ironic distance. Her tone toward

Stephen very much resembles that of William James in regard to religious mystics—sympathy mingled with pragmatic skepticism.[23] In a review of Simone Weil's essays, Oates expresses her views on religious mystics in general and her objections to Simone Weil in particular, providing us with an instructive and orienting source for understanding Stephen, though she is more sympathetic to Stephen than she is to Weil.

There is no reason, of course, for us to doubt that the mystics' ideas about the universe are objectively true. But there is no reason for us to believe that they are true. The mystic experiences a powerful subjective reorganization of his psyche, and the experience is certainly valid. But that it has reference to an entity casually called The Universe is extremely doubtful. One reads Weil, then, with a variety of emotions. Fascination at first. Exasperation. Disappointment. Even anger at her willfulness, her refusal to recognize her own narcissism though she is quick to see it in others . . . . In the end one feels a certain suspense, as in the reading of a good novel: will the heroine wake from her delusion in time to save her life?[24]

Oates is impatient with any self-enclosed vision, any vision that is exclusive and that aggrandizes the self even if the form of self-aggrandizement is self-negation. Indeed there is an element of narcissism in Stephen's mysticism. Allowing for the fact that Andrew is himself deluded, his evaluation of Stephen, though exaggerated, is nevertheless valid: "You say every human being is a miracle, Stephen . . . but what you mean is that you yourself are a miracle, the center of a miracle, and you invest the world with your transfigured vision; you give birth to the world, you and only you."

Oates probably modelled Stephen's conversion dream—which he experiences at the age of twelve and which results in a "subjective reorganization of his psyche"—on those described in *The Varieties of Religious Experience*.[25] When he comes of age, he declares himself "free of all merely human, entangling alliances," gives up his claim to his inheritance, renounces the Episcopal faith of his family, and joins the Jesuits, "filled to the brim with God." But he outgrows his "infatuation" with the Jesuits, characterizing their beliefs as "magic," not religion, and their Christ as a "fantasy." After a brief connection with the radical movements of the 60s, he attaches himself to various charitable communities as a teacher, satisfied to live in anonymity with his visions.

However, Stephen's idyllic life of good works and visionary experiences is curtailed by "the details of the finite and the immediately given," by Andrew's death that forces him back into the complex circle of his family. At one point he declares that "Paradise was continually expelling him." In fact, the visionary gift, which insulated him from the rest of humanity, begins to implicate him, to draw him into the arena of responsibility and guilt. Oates describes the deterioration of Stephen's monism as paralleling his increasing feelings of guilt. In giving up his secular ties for God, Stephen had "surrendered everything but his innocence," and Oates depicts the reversal of that process as a giving up of innocence. He has foreboding dreams in which Hugh and Andrew call him for help. When he visits his brothers, they deride him, question his sanity, and so prick his self-esteem with insults that he leaves without being able to sound a warning. When Andrew's death and Hugh's paralysis follow in quick succession, his convictions begin to erode, and finally Stephen comes to the point where he feels "God had withdrawn" from him.

Oates portrays Stephen's disillusionment in a

series of short, juxtaposed scenes in which he is pictured with Andrew, Yvonne, Hugh, and Kevin, a retarded, obese adolescent whose care and education he has made his special undertaking. In some sections, one scene glides into another, and we realize that the scenes are versions of each other but with a different character opposing Stephen's offer of salvation. Each of the episodes culminates in Stephen's rejection and failure, with him unable to penetrate the separating barriers of personality.

Oates opposes Stephen's fantasy that everything is filled with divinity by summoning wildly brutal images of facticity with which she confronts him. One is Hugh in his hospital room. Another is Kevin, "a young giant: nearly seven feet tall. Hulking, fat-thighed. Odor of armpits, crotch, soiled clothing . . . . His head was small for his body, and hairless—the pale, lard-colored skull was covered only by a fine white fuzz." For a while, Stephen sustains his conviction that Kevin, too, is God: "God squatted and hopped clumsily about and hunched his shoulders and screwed up his fat floury-pale face." But in this, too, he fails: "God departed from Stephen with a swift, sickening wrench; he was left staring at the hideously ugly face of a freakish child-giant, whom he loathed with every particle of his being." He is left faced with his impotence, to which, unlike the other characters, he accommodates: "One must make the attempt to live, after all."

The development of Stephen's character illustrates the William Jamesian perception that the world cannot be "experienced all at once in its absolute totality," that "the absolute sum total of things may never be actually experienced . . . and that a disseminated, distributed, or incompletely unified appearance is the only form that reality may yet have achieved."[26] Oates thrusts Stephen into the

entangling net of human relationships in order to
demonstrate that the perfection of a vision, of "a
reality," is an ineffectual means of dealing with an
indeterminate universe, that chaos cannot be ordered though it must be lived with. Stephen is defeated by the exclusiveness of his vision, which he
thought could account for everything but which dis-
integrated into the irrelevant when he attempted a
real engagement with facticity. His defeat results
from his final inability to dissociate himself from
the world. Unlike Weil, "he wakes from his delusion
in time to save his life." The climactic scene in Stephen's section is an apocalyptic dream-vision that
begins with "Sorry,/Sorry," and that consists of a
babble of voices, in which is intermingled transformed passages from St. John's Revelation, the
Upanishads, and an accusing, bantering demotic
voice.[27] The dream, brilliant in the sheer artistry of
its orchestration, expresses Stephen's confusion and
guilt as he loses confidence in the vision that had
ordered his world and is left at the mercy of the
manifold.

In effect, Oates suggests that monism results in
the "assassination" of reality: Hugh denies civilization; Yvonne denies love; Stephen denies the external world. Morever, the degree to which these
characters are out of touch with the life process is
depicted by their abnormal sexuality. Hugh is impotent; Yvonne is frigid; Stephen is celibate. In
their obsessive drive to capture eternity, they miss
the transience and flux that to Oates is the true
eternity. What Oates says of D. H. Lawrence may
be applied to her own vision as well. "He can experience the eternal *in* the temporal, and he realizes, as few people do, that the temporal is eternal
by its very nature . . . ."[28] Oates has inherited D. H.
Lawrence's sense of America, which he expressed

when he accused the classic American writers of an obsession with wanting to "know." He warns that "*Knowing* and *Being* are opposite, antagonistic states. The more you know, exactly, the less you *are*. The more you *are*, in being, the less you know. This is the greatest cross of man, his dualism. The blood-self, and the nerve-brain self. Knowing, then, is the slow death of being . . . . The goal is to know how not-to-know."[29] With her monists, Oates is pointing to the same American delusion and insisting on a very similar cure.

9

The Victory of Eros:
Childwold

The Assassins depicts a nightmarish world dominated by Thanatos. Oates portrays the stubborn refusal to compromise the particular absolute understanding on which the mind has fastened as a form
of death. In battling the absolutists of this time,
William James wrote: "Pluralistic empiricism knows
that everything is in an environment, a surrounding
world of other things, and that if you leave it to work
there it will inevitably meet with friction and opposition from its neighbors. Its rivals and enemies
will destroy it unless it can buy them off by .com-
promising some part of its original pretentions."[1] It
is this aversion to "buying off" the "surrounding
world of other things," really a helpless, inevitable
aversion borne of an inherited, almost instinctual,
blindness to the palpable, that drives Andrew,
Yvonne, and Hugh on their downward journey.

If Thanatos dominates *The Assassins*, it is a
ruthless and inexorable Eros that triumphs in *Childwold* (1976).[2] Oates finds little that is celebratory in
the perception that the mind's yearning for a final
understanding is futile. Thus when she focuses on
the metamorphic cycle of life itself, as she does in
Childwold, she depicts it as encroaching and relentless. In this world, then, the victorious are those

who do not attempt to wrest a sacred territory for
their own.

The world of *Childwold* is a muted and ame-
liorated world. The unexpected comes not as cataclysmic events, but as an inevitable consequence
of the natural processes of time, as puberty, the first
menstrual cycle, old age, death, the seasons suc-
ceeding one another, the dwindling of fortunes, the
burgeoning of the new and the decay of the old.
Moreover, the range of characters, though broad, is
not extreme. There are no megalomaniacs on the
order of Marvin Howe or passive narcissists like the
initial Elena (*Do With Me What You Will*). But if
Oates here discards some of her bold, sensational
devices, she does so in order to reaffirm her vision
from a shifted perspective.

As in many of her other novels, Oates portrays
the deflation of a Faustian figure, Fitz John Kasch,
but unlike the ersatz Fausts in some of her other
works, Kasch is a highly sympathetic character, and
we view his delusions and his demise with much
compassion. He is a middle-aged intellectual, a man
of ideas, who longs for a creed to live by. He is a
bolder, more adventurous Prufrock, a purer Herzog,
though less resilient and with fewer resources. We
do not feel so much the justness of his final failure
as its regrettable inevitability, for Oates in this novel
focuses on the vulnerability of all things human to
the transforming assaults of time, to the rhythmic,
transmuting, metamorphic force of the life cycle.
The most frail, the most vulnerable is the endeavor
to live by ideas without, as James saw, a concomitant
ability to compromise them when they are attacked
by "the surrounding world of other things." Indeed,
in lyric and incantatory prose, Oates compels this
surrounding world to loom as a threat to the human
drama at its center. The swelling river, the invading

vegetation, the yammering birds, the cacophony of insects, and especially the darting, ever-present children presage decay and death to all that is mature, to all that seems complete and consummate.

The novel is for Oates a nostalgic return to the rural landscape of earlier novels, the Eden Valley of *With Shuddering Fall* and *Wonderland,* a world that, according to Oates, represents the environs of Millerport, New York, where she grew up. *Childwold* is a rural village outside of Yewville, a town we recognize from *Wonderland.* The graveyard there contains markers for the Reveres, minor characters in *With Shuddering Fall* and major characters in *A Garden of Earthly Delights.* The river that marks a boundary of Joseph Hurley's property has the same mystical pull as the river in *The Assassins.* But more important, the characters indicate Oates's renewed interest in her earlier portraits, although with resurrection comes a psychological deepening. In this she resembles Henry James who, with each ressurrection of the innocent American and the corrupt European, added a deeper layer to their characterization. It is as if Oates, emerging from the hellish terrain of *The Assassins,* returns to her roots in order to reevaluate and reaffirm her world.

Arlene Bartlett, a poor, rural, lusty middle-aged widow with a series of lovers, each of whom leaves her with a child as a gratifying token of the relationship, is a more likeable Loretta (*them*), a fleshing out of "the woman in red shorts" (*The Assassins*). In one scene she is wearing "tight-fitting red slacks." She has a vitality and élan Loretta lacks. In addition, she is not as facilely forgiving of brutality, and she is more confident of her abilities. She has a stronger sense of self and is not cowed by gossip; by the haughty matrons of small-town aristocracy who staff the charity, second-hand clothes store Ar-

lene patronizes; by the violent anger of a jealous
boyfriend; or by the intrusive questions of the wel-
fare worker who eyes Arlene's belly suspiciously for
signs of another pregnancy. Arlene is a mother-earth
figure; she is like James Joyce's Molly Bloom in her
sexual appetite and like Dylan Thomas's Polly
Garter in her naturalness. She finds rhapsodic contentment in pregnancy: "How she loved it, her entire body filled and throbbing slow with life, it did
not matter that the men deserted her, that they died,
killed themselves in car wrecks and had no insurance and no savings and no thought of her—it did
not matter: only this mattered, and she had it."
Unencumbered by ideas or delusions or exceptional
ambitions, she regards her physicality with joy. She
is Oates's life-affirmer; in terms of suitability, the
perfect inhabitant of a pluralistic universe.

Two of her children figure prominently in the
narrative. Vale is a re-creation of Shar (*With Shuddering Fall*). His violent, sinister rebelliousness is
the consequence of both his nature and the nurture
of the Vietnam War, in which he suffered wounds
that leave him scar-faced and wracked with inter-
mittent pain, dependent on drugs for relief. Four-
teen-year-old Evangeline, nicknamed "Laney," is
reminiscent of the child-women protagonists who
are so prevalent in Oates's work. She may be com-
pared to Karen (*With Shuddering Fall*) and Clara
(*A Garden of Earthly Delights*) although she is more
clearly adolescent than either of them, and she has
neither Karen's ambivalent passions nor Clara's
materialistic strivings. She is more unformed than
they are, tentatively testing her newly won womanhood and searching toward individuation.

Arlene's father, "Grandpa" Joseph Hurley, is
an old man who lives within his memories, a trait
of Clara's father, Carleton. He has the silence and

dignity and stubbornness of Jesse's Grandfather Vogel (*Wonderland*). Like Carleton and Jesse's father, he is a victim of the Depression that forced the ruinous sale of the best of his proud 250-acre farm, but he is not so much bitter as he is mournful, nostalgic, and preoccupied with death and the dead. However, what distinguishes these characters most from those whom they resemble is the fact that they remain rooted to a family, a house, and a piece of land.[3]

In contrast, Fitz John Kasch, the central character, exists in a kind of limbo, feeling detached from the familiar—from his roots, from his academic Cambridge life, and like some other of Oates's pilgrims, from history. A nearsighted, brooding scholar, he returns to the carriage house on his family's estate—their mansion is now a museum—having been, despite therapy, unable to locate himself after his divorce, which was prompted by his discovery that his wife was having an affair out of boredom and convenience. The pure-hearted Kasch, aghast at her insensitivity and casualness, sinks into a despair from which he cannot arise. He returns to Yewville in confusion, hoping to construct a life for himself with the help of the books he has brought with him, or failing that, hoping to summon the courage for suicide. Although he tests various definitions of himself—poet, pervert, hero, pilgrim, voyeur—he recoils dissatisfied. In this state of bewilderment, he accidentally meets Laney by rescuing her from the crude taunts of her wine-besotted companions. His obsession becomes to possess her, overcome her, imagining that through possession he can reclaim a lost innocence, transcend a jaded and confused middle age, retreat to a state in which death is not so inviting. His desire for a complete spiritual possession is of course unfulfillable, and he tries to approximate it by attempting, unsuccessfully, to become her lover, her benefactor, her father. He imagines raping her, murdering her, and in a gentler moment, reinventing her as a character in a story. He says, "I must *know* her." Although they search, they can find no common ground for union, certainly not, like Nabokov's Humbert and Lolita, in sex. He can only yearn and she only offer bewildered sympathy.

In fact, *Childwold* is a reimagining of Nabokov's *Lolita*. Oates has previously reworked the material of other artists. Some excellent Oatesian "revisions" may be found in her short story volume, *Marriages and Infidelities,* in which she reworks, for example, James Joyce's "The Dead," Henry James's "The Turn of the Screw," and Franz Kafka's "The Metamorphosis."[4] Although *Childwold,* like *Lolita,* describes a middle-aged intellectual's infatuation with a pubescent girl, Oates transforms the characters, plot, point of view, and imagery to suit her own vision. Oates does not regard her characters and their predicament from Nabokov's Olympian heights. Her treatment is comparably realistic and even lyrical, but it is not farcical and ironic. In fact, her novel is another development in her quarrel with Nabokov, whom she sees as one of a number of "solipsistic" writers. In the *New York Times Book Review* for June 4, 1972, Oates asks: "Why is it that our cleverest writers. . . have followed so eagerly the solipsistic examples of Nabokov, Beckett, and, more recently and most powerfully, Borges?"[5] Perhaps a clearer articulation of her disagreement with Nabokov, as well as others, may be found in her statement, "Nabokov . . . [has] mastered art forms in which language is arranged and rearranged in such a manner as to give pleasure to the artist and his readers, excluding any referent to an available exterior world . . . . The consciousness discernable behind the works of Nabokov . . . is self-created, self-named, untouched by parental or social or cultural or even biological determinants."[6]

Oates's interest in *Lolita* probably centers on the fact that, although Humbert manages to elude the larger world for a time and manages to manipulate the world so that it conforms to his obsession, his confrontation with it at the end is, in Aristotle's sense, necessary and inevitable. Thus in her reworking of the novel, the necessity and inevitability of the larger world become the central theme. She creates a version of Nabokov's solipsist in Kasch and places him in James's pluralistic universe. In shifting the point of view among the characters rather than restricting it to Kasch, as Nabokov restricts it to Humbert, Oates renders Kasch as one urgent voice among several. Thus his voice, unlike Humbert's, is put into a judgmental context. The effect Oates achieves is one of perspective. When the solipsist's voice is put in an environment of other voices and when his self-enclosed universe is put in the environment of the world at large, the force of his vision is greatly diminished.

Nabokov's characters are for the most part stock figures, flat characters. Even Humbert, the protagonist, is reduced to a single passion. Oates's characters, on the other hand, are rounded and realistic. She does not reduce even Kasch, the monist, to a single characteristic. She refuses to compromise realism in this work because her subject *is* the manifest world. Unlike Humbert, who is pathologically calculating and single-minded, Kasch is sincere, overly complex, a victim of his fluctuating and warring impulses. Moreover, although Laney and Lolita enjoy some similar adolescent pleasures—for example, the reading of pulp magazines—Laney is

many-faceted, fully human, not a caricature like
Nabokov's blithe, selfish, mindless nymphet. Ar-
lene, too, is a sharp contrast to the dull philistine,
Mrs. Haze.

Additionally, Oates reverses the order in which
the protagonist becomes entangled with the mother
and the daughter. Kasch meets Arlene when, with
maternal solicitude, she visits him in order to de-
termine the nature of his interest in her daughter.
Having found the daughter elusive, he embraces
instead the mother. Although Humbert is driven by
the single lust for Lolita from the beginning, Kasch
is in search of such a "lust" in order to bring to rest
his yearning and homelessness. Arlene, like Mrs.
Haze, imagines herself as his proper bride; she is
nearer to him in age and sees in Kasch a gentle sav-
ior who is willing to love her and her children and
not unimportantly to spend his money lifting them
out of poverty. Further, he plans to buy back the
acres that the Hurley's lost during the Depression.
In other words, he plans to retrieve the past, redeem
it, and in doing so, possess a world.

His engagement with his real situation, with the
real Arlene, with the reality of a fiancée who never
finished high school, who is more promiscuous than
this ex-wife, is minimal. Kasch obfuscates the harsh
realities with his lyrical and objectifying imagination. He does not evoke for himself a picture of
"Arlene" and "Kasch" but rather chants of "The
Bride and The Bridegroom." His is a fragile delusion maintained by enormous effort, which his frequent migraine headaches betray. It is a delusion
whose destruction Oates has made implicit before
she lets it fully form in the mind of her character,
foreshadowed in Kasch's personal history, in the
plot, as well as in the structure of motifs and imagery.

Indeed, although he claims to be "enchanted," first with the daughter and then with the mother, all of his acts are determined and underwritten by an idea, for what is an enchantment but the surrender of the real for an idea? He cannot accept even Laney in her manifoldness; he feels revulsion when he contemplates her poverty and what he sees as her probable destiny, preferring to think of her as detached from her real universe, existing as an idea in his mind. Echoing Humbert, he describes Laney as his "own invention," his "own treasure."[7]

As in Fitzgerald's *The Great Gatsby*, Jay Gatsby's romance is with money, Kasch's romance is with ideas. In a passage that closely echoes a passage from Thoreau, who himself is an example of an American monist who, in retreating to Walden, tried to reduce and thereby control a world, Kasch states:

I returned to Yewville, scene of my birth, because I wished to live deliberately, to retreat from history, both personal and collective . . . . I wanted to live deep and suck out all the marrow of life, as the saying goes, to drive life into a corner and reduce it to its lowest terms.[8]

Oates strews his interior monologus with conflicting philosophic ideas that serve as an index of his confusion. His quarrel with the experiential is that it fades into history, that it does not last. He says, "Once the world slips into the past tense, once it shifts into 'history,' it is revealed to have been insubstantial; illusory; deceptive." Because life is transient, continually receding, he feels justified in denying its reality. A true reality, he feels, is invested with timelessness. Consequently, he views time and his body as traps.

In creating Kasch, Oates creates a monist with whom we can sympathize (unlike Nabokov's Humbert or the monists in *The Assassins*) and yet whose error is clear. She depicts her allegiance with William James's radical empiricism by identifying the errors in Kasch's life against a pluralistic background. One of the novel's epigraphs comes from James: "We are not the readers but the very personages of the world-drama." James felt that "we become selves through synthesizing our past, present, and future."[9] In contrast, Kasch feels he must create a self that is detached from time, that "life in time, in history" is "a failure." When he meets Laney, he describes her ideally, as "a ninety-five-pound angel" and as having saved him from the Jamesian "maggot-swarming corpse," an image of mutability. He does not acknowledge that Laney, too, is in time, that she is part of the "maggot-swarming corpse."

In her protagonist's interior monologues, Oates depicts his decreasing grasp of the "surrounding world of other things." Although his observations are sometimes lucid, the conclusions he draws from them violate the empirical world he observes. Rather than accept the experiential, he denies its reality. "A common misconception I once wanted to write about in depth: that human life is centered upon and determined by events. On the contrary, the interior life constitutes the authentic life, and actions performed in the exterior world are peripheral. Reality is what I am thinking . . . ." Kasch is an Oatesian post-Renaissance man who leaps to solipsism because he assumes that there is a Truth and that this Truth, now that God is dead, resides in the self.

His quest is, in fact, godlike: to invent, embrace, and contain the world. He says, "A land glimpsed for the first time in the hard, overexposed clarity of dreams: a land waiting to be claimed, to be possessed by the dreamer. Kingly and triumphant. The

dreamer wakes, the dreamer steps forth." Perplexed
by the pluralistic, he claims to be the One. In an
inverted echo of James's rhetorical question, "How
can what is manifold be one?" he says, "Am I not
the One who controls the many . . . ? I bear the
world, yes, but I am far from lost in it!"[10]

As with Stephen, whom in his gentleness Kasch
most resembles, Oates depicts his chastening as an
encounter with the physical, with facticity, in the
form of Earl, Arlene's former lover. Earl, who lurks
in the background throughout the novel, is the an-
tithesis of Kasch. Strong, burly, pugilistic, he is the
man of action, jealous of his territorial rights. After
a tawdry scene in which he beats Arlene in a drunken rage, she repeatedly refuses his attentions.
When he returns to Childwold in order to reassert
his claim on Arlene, he finds the intruder, Kasch.
They battle, and although Kasch is victorious, his
victory comes at the cost of Earl's life, a cost that his
sanity cannot bear. His victory is highly ironic, for
the body he hoped to transcend is what he instinctively preserves. In Oates's world one always comes
up hard against the urgency of the physical; life is
distilled into the palpable, the real, the experiential.
In her portrayal of Kasch, Oates not only exposes
the false dichotomy of mind and body, but indicates
that the Western proclivity for this dichotomy is a
symptom of a larger falsification, the idea that the
right application of mind wins immortality, for
Kasch's attempt to idealize his existence is nothing
if not an attempt to escape time.

In the confrontation between Kasch and Childwold, Oates awakens us to the ineluctable reality
of the physical world. His descent into the eerily
enchanting Childwold is the descent of the man of
ideas into the primordial world where the relentless
flow of the life cycle, not masked by the artifacts of

civilization, is revealed in all of its power. By immersing him in a universe ruled by natural processes, Oates creates an emblem of Faustian futility.

Oates's controlling metaphor for the coursing of organic life is metamorphosis, a metaphor she has transposed from *Lolita*. Alfred Aspel, Jr., describes its significance in Nabokov's work: "Just as the nymph undergoes a metamorphosis in becoming the butterfly, so everything in *Lolita* is constantly in the process of metamorphosis, including the novel itself—a set of 'notes' being compiled by an imprisoned man during a fifty-six day period for possible use at his trial, emerging as a book after his death, and then only after it has passed through yet another stage, the nominal 'editorship' of John Ray, Jr. As Lolita turns from a girl into a woman, so Humbert's lust becomes love . . . ."[11] However, in the enlarged world of *Childwold*, the metaphor is literally universalized, not restricted to the fictional process and the characters, but it reaches out to include the entire physical world. Oates is dramatizing James's perception that "the essence of life is its continually changing character."[12] Indeed, the entire world of *Childwold* is undergoing a perpetual process of metamorphosis. All things are emerging from one stage and reaching toward another, directed by the flow of the life force. As in *Lolita*, the characters are in various phases, but Oates's emphasis is on biological as well as emotional metamorphosis. There is Joseph in old age, Kasch in middle age, Arlene in ripe womanhood, Vale in young manhood, Laney in adolescence, and towards the end of the novel, there is Ronnie, who is just emerging from boyhood. Lurking everywhere, though we do not often hear their voices directly, are the children, waiting in the shadows for their turn to supplant their elders.

As with *Lolita,* the butterfly is a central symbol of metamorphosis, but again Oates enlarges on Nabokov's material. With the exception of the last scene, the time span of the novel follows nearly the year of a butterfly, from September to the following July. In addition, in Oates's work, the symbol embraces the entire universal process. In the early passage, grandfather Joseph, in one of his revery-dominated dawn walks, observes the "intense butterfly-dotted" landscape and muses on the "frantic activity" of the butterfly's life cycle: "mating laying of eggs hatching of eggs larvae cocoons wriggling forth life mating death eggs mating death-cocoons, death wriggling forth . . . ." Oates ends Joseph's catalogue of the butterfly's life cycle appropriately with death because as an old man, Joseph is about to undergo his final metamorphic phase.

Laney, however, is just emerging from her cocoon, which Oates images as her attic room—a place that is "secret and cave like," a place of contentment, warmth, and safety. In fact, Laney's room, a confusion of colors and shapes, representing her as yet undifferentiated, immature state, is dominated by a "glossy photograph of a Monarch butterfly, magnified many times."

As Oates depicts Laney and Joseph in "phase," she depicts Kasch as out of phase. Kasch invokes a theory of *paedomorphosis,* "whereby the organic universe can revitalize itself indefinitely. The biological clock can be rewound, there is sometimes an escape from the cul-de-sac of evolutionary 'progress' . . . ." Although this theory has many implications in a novel in which children and other burgeoning life forms loom as a threat to mature life, it is pointed mainly at Kasch and the monistic tradition that he represents. Oates implies that the wish for personal rebirth is comparable to a wish to

rewind the biological clock.[13] By linking Kasch's
quest for personal renewal with the theory of *paedomorphosis*, the turning back of the biological
clock, Oates implies that such a quest is not only
absurd but dangerous. It is an attempt to abrogate
the fundamental biological terms of existence; the
result can only be the creation of self-destructive,
self-isolating delusionary systems. With Freudian
clarity Kasch states his pathological goal: "Kasch
becoming the father of himself. Kasch self-or-
dained." In the euphoria of marital preparation, he
declares, "I am new, I am trembling with newness,
I am like a child, I am innocent of past accomplish-
ments as well as past sins, there is no connection,
no attachment . . . ." His conviction that he is self-
created is a manifestation of the "imperial self" that
Quentin Anderson attributes to the "failure of the
fathers" of America. In speaking of Emerson, Anderson says, Emerson "too was saying that time
must have a stop, that society was unthinkable, that
history was an insult to the being of our own immediate perceptions—that we were our own fathers."[14] Kasch casts aside his beloved books, rel-
egating them to the status of artifacts of his "larval
stage." In imagining that he is his own progenitor,
he finds himself in the untenable position of having
to blink the past and the present. It is with a stroke
of cosmic irony that Oates portrays his true birth
into the world, not the objectified, idealized, undivided world of The Bride and The Bridegroom
but the physical world of Arlene and Earl. Kasch,
who wanted the impossible, is arrested by the inevitable.

As with the Petries in *The Assassins*, Oates
traces Kasch's sickness to the "failures of his fathers." Although Kasch declares himself detached
from his personal history, he is merely repeating the

errors of his forbears. His family's wealth comes
from his great-great-grandfather, who made a fortune in lumber and who won and then lost a seat
in Congress. His strong anti-Republican stand in the
1860s provoked a mob into fire-bombing his house.
He rebuilt his mansion with stone so that it would
be invulnerable to further public outrage. Kasch
describes it as a "fortress, a mausoleum." Ironically,
it is now a public museum, and the only trace of its
original owner is his name, which the museum
bears. In addition, Kasch's parents are pathetic figures who spent their lives attempting to deny their
bodies and in doing so hoped to uncover the mystery of existence. In a moment of clarity, Kasch says,
"Deny, transcend. Escape. Inherit."

For Oates the American Dream is a false dream
of conquest, control, ownership, and finally an impossible dream of overcoming mutability. She
dramatizes its futility not only in her portrait of
Kasch but also of Joseph. In his portrait, Oates re-
counts a familiar immigration story. As a child, Joseph immigrated to America, pushed from the
bosom of his family in Ireland to his childless
American uncle, a farmer. Homeless and uprooted,
Joseph proceeds to establish a world "subservient"
to him from which he cannot be ousted. He states,
"I wasn't born here in America but I am an American in my bones." And in an earlier passage, he
says, "You own all the land from the Eden River to
the Yewville Road and the village of Marsena and
all the dreaming drifting warring life within it, it's
yours, no debts, no mortgages, owned free and clear
on this day of April 16, 1921 . . . ." However, by
1976, he has difficulty in clearing even a kitchen
garden on his diminished eight-acre property as the
"drifting warring life" is reclaiming the land. As
Joseph approaches death, he cries impotently for

"A sign, a sign?"—for an explanation of his failure to outwit the Depression, the landscape, and death.

Oates juxtaposes Kasch's static, self-enclosed universe with the Childwold landscape that is in violent rhythmic motion, where wind, sky, vegetation, and river dominate. Joseph is the most articulate observer of these upheavals: "The sky rears and tosses, the sky is frightening . . . . The wind blows everything out of place." Later, as Joseph comes closer to his decision to commit suicide by plunging into the river, he describes its hypnotic movement. "Noise of it, crashing waves; always here . . . . Washing, pounding, roaring . . . . Waves, light breaking into thousands of bits, millions of bits, like stars. A living network of them quivering, singing, calling: waves, wind, voices."

In fact, our sense of order comes more from the movement of the novel through the lunar and yearly cycle than from plot development. What usually serves as background—seasons, time of day, weather—Oates pushes in the foreground so that the characters' lives mirror the universal process rather than the reverse. It is Kasch who makes us aware in turn of the approaching winter and summer solstice. At the "farthest point of the sun's retreat" Kasch's life is also in retreat: Laney eludes him, his books yield no answers, and he has not yet met Arlene. Moreover, his confrontation with Earl occurs near the summer solstice. It is as if their meeting were consonant with some universal process, necessary and inevitable not only in terms of the pressure of personality but the pressure of natural forces as well.

The moon, another symbol of metamorphosis, is for the most part associated with Laney. It is a curiously appropriate symbol for her since it implies both the chasteness of Diana and the monthly female cycle of menstruation that Laney, for whom it is a recent experience, describes in one of her interior monologues.[15] Kasch thinks of her in her "moon-haunted bed"; he first sees her in the "uncertain moonlight." She, herself, feels "likely to be brushed by the moon's light." Although Kasch and Vale are most often pictured at night, it is the night of chaos, not regulated by lunar phases. They are, in some ways, two faces of the same Janus image in that they are both estranged and out of phase with their environment, though Vale's is an estrangement by violence rather than ideas. (In fact, they go to the same prostitute.) Oates depicts the grandfather mostly at dawn, signifying the meeting of two points in the life cycle—death (the grandfather) and birth (the dawn, representing the new life that will supersede him). Arlene, on the other hand, who is in the full bloom of womanhood and the possessor of a practical intelligence, is portrayed mostly in daylight.

However, the natural world is not only tumultuous; it not only reflects and guides human life, but it encroaches. Joseph, surveying his house and property, thinks:

There's cold air rising from the floorboards . . . . Last summer there was moss on the old cow barn; and trumpet vine growing like crazy. Sunflowers and hollyhocks moving right in . . . and saplings all over.

The house and the property are two of the book's emblems signifying the implacable movement of time that pushes everything into history, making way for the future.

Not only nature, but culture is also a force of mutability. Significantly Kasch lives on *museum* grounds. (His room is littered with the carcasses of insects.) The house belonging to his Aunt Leita,

whom he visits to announce his proposed marriage,
is the last of the street's original houses, the area
having been taken over by commercial buildings.
With sardonic wit Oates has Kasch describe the
view he surveys as he faces his dowager aunt in
their tea ritual: "If I look over Aunt Leita's head and
out through the back yard I can see, beyond the
three remaining elms . . . the revolving sign from a
drive-in restaurant on the other street; I think it consists of a white bucket with a man's face on it, grin-
ning as he bites into a drumstick." Additionally,
Arlene's son, Ronnie, bored by the pageant of his
grandfather's burial, concentrates yearningly on the
jet plane that roars overhead.

Oates wins many of her effects with the form
she has chosen for the novel. It is a prose lyric to
the life process. Oates relies heavily on the techniques of poetry to evoke her world—refrain, par-
allelism, word-play, lack of narrative exposition,
lack of transitions between the shifting voices of the
characters, and repetition of key images. It is an
effective vehicle for the novel's themes of transience and the life cycle. The voices alternately melt
into, clash with, and displace one another, thus imitating the book's themes. There are whole pages
and lines devoted to word-play, to transformations
of the word "*childwold.*" Childwold is not only the
village in which the Bartletts live but the name literally means child-forest, and those two words sum-
marize the concerns of the book. The forest is a
metaphor signifying the pluralistic universe with
which the novel so richly resonates. Arlene, as an
embodiment of mother-earth, bears the children
who make the world of the novel a "child-forest."
Although her children never really emerge as individual characters (except for Ronnie), collectively

they dart, intrude, lurk, invade, tease, always on the fringes of action, seeming ready to pounce.

"The children, the children" is a refrain, and Oates uses the image to convey a sense of the supplanting of one generation by another. In fact, the image occurs in a striking and powerful short story entitled "The Children." In it, Oates traces a mother's increasing terror of her own child, who, the mother is convinced, is involved in an evil, secret plot, along with other children, that threatens her existence.[16] The last scene ends with the crazed mother beating the child until she draws blood.

In *Childwold*, the image of "the children" becomes increasingly menacing as the novel progresses. In an early passage, they are pictured as exuberant and energetic: "They bounced and giggled and burrowed beneath the covers" of Arlene's bed. A few pages later, Oates focuses on their sheer number. Laney recalls the teasing chants of her friends, *"One little, two little, three little Bartletts . . . four little, five little . . . . And another one on the way"*. In the opening passage of Part Three, written from Kasch's point of view and put on a page by itself, the image is expanded, taking on ambiguous religious and demonic associations.

The children dart into corners, into shadows; hide-and-seek in the deep crevices; your lips move in prayer, in play. Caught you! There you are! One of the children stares at you, her underlip caught in her teeth. You would plunge forward to kneel at her feet, you would stagger, you would cry aloud with joy—/Angels, demons./Cannot see them clearly.

Oates ends Part Four with an echo of this passage in which the image is associated with the river and thus change, flux, transience, and the life force:

"Playing hide-and-seek in the waves, in the light
broken in the waves. Swimming, diving, swelling,
subsiding . . . rising again to fill the world." Their
voices and presence begin to intrude aggressively
on the adult world. As Arlene and Kasch lie in bed,

Children dart into the shadowy corners of the room; a
child scrambles beneath the bed. Another is turning back
the bedcovers, carefully, reverentially . . . . You open
the closet door and one of them is crouching inside, the
hem of a dress over his face. He scrambles away on his
hands and knees, giggling . . . . They scramble out of the
shadows, they are thunderous on the stairs, the old house
shakes with their gaiety . . . .

Theirs is the joy of the victor. Moreover, even Arlene and Kasch are described as pushing aside their
elders. While Joseph stands at the river's edge, his
revery is repeatedly interrupted by Arlene's demanding "pa, pa." Kasch thinks of his marriage as
a way of supplanting his dowager aunt; he says,
"Old woman, out of my way."
    In addition, Oates uses the juxtaposition of
voices to emphasize the succession of generations.
In the sequence immediately following Joseph's
death, we hear the children's chafing banter. The
culmination of this motif occurs a few pages later
when Ronnie's voice, heard for the first time, replaces that of his dead grandfather. This image and
all that it portends is a darkly ironic contrast to
Kasch's aspirations to embrace and contain the
Childwold family. In a climactic passage, Kasch, in
an ecstatic, lyric voice claims Childwold "forever."

But no, you are not alone, you are never going to be alone
again, the woman stands before you, waiting, she has been
waiting all this time . . . . In the distance the children cry
out to you, the old man mumbles something you cannot
hear, the winds poke about the house, many-fingered cu-

rious . . . . *You hold them all in one embrace.* All. Always.
Forever./ I love—/ I—.

The passage is doubly ironic because after killing
Earl and recuperating in a mental hospital, he lives
out his life in the decaying Bartlett house, which
Arlene and her children abandon, surrounded by
the ever-encroaching vegetation and natural life
that eventually must swallow him. He ends not by
embracing Childwold but by becoming its prisoner.
The permanence that he seeks paradoxically resides
in the unstoppable power of the transient that has
dominion over everything. Although Oates portrays
Kasch with much sympathy, his destruction is not
meant as a defeat, but as a victory of Eros over Thanatos, for no matter how engaging a character he is,
for Oates, monism, whatever its form, is deathly.

   In rhapsodic prose, Oates, speaking through
Laney, who is riding a horse and experiencing menstruation, describes her sanctified universe:

Alive, alive. Everything is alive . . . . Bankside bushes,
sumac and willow, and vines trailing into the creek dry
as corn shucks, mustard weed high as your shoulder, flies
buzzing, bees everywhere . . . small white butterfly, a
water pipit walking on the other bank, a hawk cruising
slowly in the distance, . . . the minute seeping of blood . . . .
What does it mean, why did you come here? . . . a place,
another of the sacred places you will remember all your
life . . . . The air rings with life . . . . It's [menstruation]
lovely, it won't hurt, nothing will hurt for long, it's what
you must accept, it's normal, it's beautiful, it's alive, it's
living, you don't own your body, you don't own the creek,
you can't control it, you musn't try, you must float with
the current, the plunge of the rapids, you must close your
eyes and move with it, everything is spilling toward you,
around you, inside you, through you, your blood flows
with it, you are rivers and streams and creeks, there is a
heartbeat inside you, around you—.[17]

Laney, as her given name, Evageline, implies, is the inchoate evangelist of Oates's vision. Through her sensibility, Oates sets forth the central themes of her vision—that one's life can neither be "owned" nor "controlled" and that we conform to a universal "heartbeat" which we cannot transcend; therefore the only choice—Laney says "must"—is to surrender.

The last section of the novel opens with Arlene's voice. Significantly, it is the first time she opens a section of the book, thus indicating that she is Oates's survivor, the true initiate. She is on the arm of a new lover, enjoying the festivity of a fourth of July picnic, voicing regret over her loss of Kasch, but reconciled, accepting, ready to begin anew. Yet, though she views Arlene as a survivor type, Oates is unwilling to relinquish the world to her. She does not finally resolve the tension between Faust and Adam, Thanatos and Eros, Will and Being because she sees this tension as inherent in the human condition. As Kasch declares, *"Doppelgänger* not a myth . . . . Not just the mad who are split but all of us, brains split as if with an ax . . . ."* Therefore, in the last scene, Laney, who returns to Childwold to see Kasch though he has refused a meeting, observes her childhood landscape, "Eating. Devouring. Cloud into cloud, bud into blossoms into ragged shredded petals . . . . Sow thistle grown nine or ten feet high by the barn," and asks, "Is there no one to cut it back, no one to tear it out by the roots?" The manifold world appears as a seductive invitation for man to exert his power over it. Laney echoes her grandfather in the novel's final words, "A sign, a sign . . . ?" Thus, though she respects the life force, she is constrained by her inheritance and finally by the very fact of her humanity to voice this question. Laney asks for an explanation of the unresolvable conflict between man and the rest of nature.

Her call for "a sign" implies the question that if man's fate is to live perpetually in the conviction that other life forms are subordinate to him, why then is it his destiny to succumb with them to the implacable rhythm of time? The question addresses the ironic discrepancy between man's hubris and his mortality. Although Oates refuses to resolve the conflict she so forcefully dramatizes, the novel does offer an affirmation in that it depicts the life force as prevailing over this, perhaps inevitable, conflict.

10

Epilogue

From her first novel, *With Shuddering Fall* (1964), in which the adolescent heroine reembraces her father after testing her "freedom," to *Childwold* (1976), in which the protagonist ends as a prisoner of the life force he foolishly thought he could manipulate, Joyce Carol Oates's fiction affirms that man is located in a universe that he can either transcend nor control and from which there is no separation or redemption. If some classic American and some modern and contemporary writers have been unable to accept this condition—have instead taken the perilous journey into the "rebellious imperatives of the self"—Oates nevertheless has a literary predecessor who not only accepted but affirmed this condition. Frank Budgen reports that James Joyce asked him, "Do you know of any complete all-round character presented by any writer?" When Budgen offered Goethe's Faust, Joyce replied, "Faust! . . . Far from being a complete man, he isn't a man at all. Is he an old man or a young man? Where are his home and family? . . . No-age Faust isn't a man."[1] Joyce's choice, as we well know, is Ulysses, a man with a wife, a son, and a home—a "complete" man. As this study has attempted to show, Oates shares this sense of "completion." In her fiction and in her criticism she proposes the image of the associated

life, which "completion" implies, as a healing alternative to the image of Faust, with which our culture has for so long been infatuated. In her novels,
Oates pursues the American Faust through rural,
urban, and surburban America; she depicts him in
the guise of a man, a woman, an adolescent, and a
child; as a race-car driver, a migrant-worker's
daughter, a writer, a doctor, a lawyer, a politician,
a caricaturist, a religious mystic, and an intellectual.
He seems, in Oates's fiction, to be an inevitable and
apparently inexorcizable part of the American soul.
And as a manifestation of Thanatos, as a tempter
who offers the seductions of darkness, of death, he
seems an inevitable and apparently inexorcizable
part of the psyche. In Oates's fiction, as in the psyche, he is locked in eternal bottle with the life force.
What is perhaps unique about Joyce Carol Oates as
an American writer is not that Faust's defeat is depicted as inevitable, but that his defeat is depicted
as necessary, that it is affirmed, however qualified
and painful that affirmation may be.

Just as Oates insists that her protagonists exist
in an environment of "other things," she insists that
her art is not the independent product of an isolated
effort, but that her fiction is "the creation of thousands upon thousands of processes of conscious
ness."[2] The "isolated artist," she declares, is a
"myth." This accounts for the numerous allusions
in her work (the Bible, the Upanishads, Joyce, Beckett, Nabokov, Thoreau, D. H. Lawrence, William
James, Sylvia Plath, Lewis Carroll, Wordsworth—
to name only a few that this study and others have
identified), the translation of other artistic visions
into her own idiom, and her interest in literary criticism; and it bespeaks her profound commitment to
a philosophy of community.

The dominant impressions with which one

comes away from a study of Oates's fiction are of its unity, of an artist who is continually refining her craft, and of a vision that, though unified, is very much in process. From a chronological study of the novels, there emerges a clear sense of the author's developing artistry. The movement in Oates's art is from raw, powerful, catacylsm-packed novels to subtler, more complex, self-conscious vehicles; from a dependence on plot to a dependence on form.

Oates's first two novels, *With Shuddering Fall* and *A Garden of Earthly Delights,* are written with a traditional third-person point of view, linear development, and full narrative exposition. In *With Shuddering Fall*, Oates employs a combination of the omniscient and limited-omniscient narrator. Although this combination is relied upon in *A Garden of Earthly Delights*, Oates artfully uses the limited-omniscient point of view, for the most part filtering the story through, respectively, Carleton, Clara, and Swan, after whom the three sections of the novel are named. *Expensive People* is, of course, a first-person narrative, a point of view that Oates uses with great effect in many of her short stories. (Indeed, even in early short stories, she repeatedly conducts experiments in form.) Although the first-person narrative is a traditional angle of vision, Oates's use of it in an early novel is unusual since the three novels which follow it—*them, Wonderland,* and *Do With Me What You Will*—are told from the third-person point of view.

In her later novels, Oates masterfully integrates form and content. As a result, her later work offers a fiction that is less immediately penetrable by the reader than the vivid, forceful, event-filled early novels. Yet the later fiction provides a richer texture for the reflective reader to contemplate. With each novel, Oates relies less heavily on traditional modes.

Although *Wonderland* also depends on third-person narration and linear development, the novel's structure—the layering of the motifs of history, religion, evolution, philosophy, and oral, womb, and distorted human body imagery, as well as the use the novel makes of Carroll's Alice tales—indicates the author's increased interest in the novel as artifact, as aesthetic object.

Do With Me What You Will, for instance, represents an experiment in both point of view and narrative form. The omniscient and limited-omniscient narration is often interspersed with italicized passages of a character's interior monologue, sometimes, as in the case of Shelley and Mered Dawe, in an epistolary form. In addition, Oates abandons linear development in the first half of the novel: The first book of the novel relates the history of Elena up to the moment that she meets Jack, and the second book, concerned largely with the same time period, relates the history of Jack up to the moment that he meets Elena. Once they meet, the novel proceeds more or less linearly. Additionally in this novel, Oates weds form with theme. The legal metaphor we recall, is sewn into the structural fabric of the novel, with each of the book's sections corresponding to a part of a trial.

In *The Assassins* and *Childwold*, Oates makes further use of formal strategies to bear thematic weight. As a result, she accomplishes an even more intimate union between form and theme. In fact, one may say that form *is* theme in these novels. The monistic absolutists who populate the world of *The Assassins* are revealed through their streams of consciousness. Each consciousness is isolated from the others in a separate section of the novel, just as each character is isolated from the living totality of being by virtue of his stubborn adherence to a personal version of reality. Although each of the characters rehearses the events of the same historical period, each rehearsal portrays a radically different drama, reflecting the delusions of the main actor of that section of the novel. Moreover, each section is underpinned with imagery appropriate to the voice that controls that section.

In *Childwold*, Oates artfully manipulates the voices so that their very sequence imitates the novel's thematic preoccupations. *The Assassins* makes some limited use of the third-person narrator, but in *Childwold*, Oates completely abandons narrative omniscience and instead relies on the techniques of poetry to develop her drama and to convey a sense of structure and unity. Every aspect of the novel—the structure, the tonal modulations, the biological and emotional state of the characters, the shifting points of view, the underpinning with William Jamesian pluralism—contributes to what Henry James termed "the handsome wholeness of effect."[3] These last two novels, especially, are compelling illustrations of Oates's mature artistic powers.

Despite the versatility of Joyce Carol Oates's imagination, which provides us with fictions that have such diverse subject matter as law, medicine, politics, and religion and such diverse settings as farms, small towns, cities, and suburbias, Oates continually reworks her material. The perversely playful confessional tone of the narrator's voice in *Expensive People*, for example, is repeated in the voice of Trick in *Wonderland* and the voice of Hugh in *The Assassins*. In *Childwold* the novel's characters and setting are reminiscent of earlier portraits and settings. In the same way that Laney is another version of Oates's adolescent heroine and Arlene is a fuller portrait of Loretta (*them*) and the woman in red shorts (*The Assassins*), Kasch is a synthesis of

the portraits of Max (*With Shuddering Fall*), Lowry
(*A Garden of Earthly Delights*), Geffen (*them*), Dr.
Pedersen (*Wonderland*), Howe (*Do With Me What
You Will*) and Stephen (*The Assassins*), all of whom
suffer from hubris and a misdirected intelligence.

Oates reworks her imagery as well, and if we
trace the image of pregnancy—an important and
pervasive image in the Oates cannon—and related
images through her novels, we gain an additional
appreciation of her evolving craftsmanship and an
understanding of the direction of her art. Each of
Oates's early novels depicts an actual pregnancy.
However, as Oates reworks the image in successive
novels, it begins to serve a purely metaphorical
function, and finally, in *Childwold*, it is transformed
into a symbol of the life force.

Oates's development as an artist is marked by
her increasing awareness of the possibilities of imagery and symbol. Although the image of pregnancy
has metaphorical significance throughout the novels, the image has an increasingly deeper, more abstract phychological and philosophical resonance in
the later works. The first novel's heroine, Karen
Herz, suffers a miscarriage, signifying her miscarried love for Shar and her miscarried attempt to gain
freedom; Clara is most fulfilled when she is pregnant with Swan; Nada planned to abort Richard
when she was pregnant with him, just as she plans
to abort him from her emotional life; the final Maureen posits her baby against the terror of the outside
world; her pregnancy serves as proof of her acceptance of ordinary life.

However, in *Wonderland*, as we have seen, the
image takes on a highly metaphorical function. Although only Helene is actually pregnant, all of the
female characters have something to say about their
wombs. Their attitude toward their wombs and

pregnancy is, in fact, a measure of their relationship to the external world; the womb, here, is a metaphor for self-insulation, for the introverted libido. The image is pointed directly at the larger issues with which the novel concerns itself. Although no actual pregnancy is depicted in *Do With Me What You Will*, Elena's recovery from passivity, her birth into time and into love is, we recall, described in terms of a pregnancy. The image implies the division of the self, the giving of oneself to another, which is the novel's overriding preoccupation.

The image plays a lesser role in *The Assassins*, in which it is restricted to Yvonne's section: Yvonne has a miscarriage; she repeatedly speaks in terms of abortion; and her menstrual cycle is irregular—all symptoms of her overvaluation of the faculty of intellect. However, in *Childwold*, the image is pervasive, all-encompassing, and generalized in the depiction of the life force. It takes on a cluster of associations: it is applied not only to the fertile Arlene and her fertile older daughter, Nancy, but to the fertility of the whole order of nature, which supplants old forms with new, making way for the future. Fertility, pregnancy, children, new plant life, even new cultural forms are all emblems of the implacable movement of time, which levels all human endeavors in moving through its eternal cycle of birth, maturation, and death.

Although it would perhaps be hasty to do so, one may almost speak of "periods" in Oates's art. Reviewers of the early novels were alternately fascinated and repulsed by the violent plots and the largely inarticulate, acted-upon protagonists (though Richard in *Expensive People*, who is highly articulate, is an exception). Understandably, they responded to the visceral images these novels offer. In these early novels, the philosophical preoccupations are almost overshadowed by the intense, turbulent energy their plots radiate. Oates's first novel, *With Shuddering Fall,* seems almost to resist its author's metaphysical concerns. With what seems insistence, Oates creates the minor character Max to voice the novel's philosophical statements because such statements would be inappropriate in the mouth of either Karen or Shar. And as reviewers of the early novels complained of the violent plots, reviewers of the later novels complained of an over-subtle development and an overly rich prose. In these attacks on the later novels we hear echoed the attacks on Henry James's late works and with the same degree of justice or irrelevance.

Oates's early novels move largely by a succession of catastrophic events, which dictate to a significant degree the direction of a character's development. The author offers the characters either loaded alternatives or no alternative. Karen, for instance, must either go with Shar or remain forever a child absolutely dependent on her father; Maureen may choose either to marry Randolph or to live in continual danger of disintegration.

Although the pressure that the external world exerts is a central tenet of Oates's vision—that is, in Oates's fiction, as stated previously, man is always viewed in the perspective of the larger world—the nature of this pressure changes. For example, the number and type of violent events portrayed in *With Shuddering Fall* is comparable to the number and type portrayed in *Childwold.* In the first novel there are accidents, beatings, a suicide, and a race riot, and each of these events functions to move the characters through the novel. In *Childwold,* too, there are a beating, a fatal accident, a suicide, and a murder, but they do not dominate the fiction to the extent that such events dominate in the earlier novels. The pressure of personality rather than events, per se, becomes much more significant. Although Kasch's final chastening is a result of his confrontation with the physical world, his downfall is impelled more by his own confusion, by his own complexity and misguided desires, than by any outside pressures.

In the earlier works, especially *With Shuddering Fall, A Garden of Earthly Delights, them,* and *Wonderland,* the individual's aspirations are continually thwarted by a universe in which accident dominates; but in *The Assassins* and *Childwold,* it is the life force itself that the characters futilely challenge by attempting to impose their monistic versions of reality on it. Thus, although the external world is still portrayed as capricious and contingent in the later works as in the earlier ones, it is depicted in the later works as having a direction and design to which all of nature conforms.

This change in the depiction of the external world suggests an altered tone in the fiction, a more affirmative and encompassing vision of reality. The life force transcends the deluded and deathly attempts of the ego to control and incorporate the world; it imbues the individual's life with purposefulness; and it restores the universe to coherence. The life force gives a sense of immutability to the mutable and of timelessness to the transient.

Yet this affirmation is not unqualified. As the final scene of *Childwold* illustrates, Oates is unwilling finally to resolve the conflict, which she believes the Renaissance to have bequeathed to us, between the ego and the larger world. In her portraits of the religious mystics, Mered Dawe and Stephen Petrie, Oates entertains the possibility of per-

sonal transcendence, and although she defeats both
of these characters, their presence in the novels
slightly dwarfs the dramas of the other characters.

Her fullest exploration of religious mysticism
is in *Son of the Morning*, published too late for a
lengthy consideration here, which concerns a Pentecostal preacher. From the opening sequence in
which a savage and ravenous pack of abandoned
dogs threaten lives and livestock in a rural upstate
New York community to the closing sequence in
which Nathan Vickery, defeated Pentecostal
preacher, former head of the Church of the Seekers,
waits beseechingly for God's word, *Son of the
Morning* speaks of hunger. The physical hunger of
the dogs, whom Oates describes as pure stomach,
"a certain length of guts about which the animal
skeleton and flesh moved," prepares us for the just
as palpable spiritual hunger of the hero, Nathan
Vickery. Although the hunger to overcome human
limitation is Oates's abiding theme, nowhere does
Oates develop this theme with such single-mind-
edness as in *Son of the Morning*. She creates a protagonist who is so sure of his inner voice that the
novel's minor characters do not significantly affect
his actions or decisions. Rather they are incidental,
and all of their attempts to influence, even to kill
him, not only fail, but are simply irrelevant, gratuitous gestures. Unlike Ahab, who depends on the
communal effort of his crew to keep his world afloat,
Nathan Vickery believes himself singularly independent of all—all, that is, except God, the object
of his hunger. Of course, it is just this hunger that
cannot be satisfied.

As the dogs' physical hunger corresponds to
Vickery's spiritual hunger, so does the physical rape
of Vickery's mother, Elsa, which leaves her pregnant at the age of fifteen with Nathan, correspond

to the seven spiritual "rapes," the violent mystical possessions (the first at the age of five) of Nathan by the Divine Spirit. And although Vickery feels privileged because of these experiences, feels he is chosen by God to preach His Word, the "Spirit of the Lord" always departs, leaving him physically exhausted, somewhat confused, and yearning anew.

Despite the fact that Vickery's obsession renders him oblivious to the events and people around him, Oates has brought to life a whole population infected with Pentecostal fever. There is Vickery's grandmother who manages his upbringing and who turns away from her general practitioner husband, the novel's "man of reason," for the Pentecostal church to which she introduces her religiously precocious grandson. There is the vulgar Leonie Beloff, daughter of the successful and hypocritical Reverend Beloff, who tempts Vickery's flesh. There is Japheth, the scholar, who comes to a meeting of the Seekers ostensibly out of boredom, but is so transfixed by Vickery's preaching that he gives up his former life to follow the Seekers. There are the hundred, then the thousands, and when Vickery's reputation becomes national and he preaches over radio and television, the hundreds of thousands who not only give him their faith, but their money as well. But Oates is not re-creating Elmer Gantry; Vickery is genuine. He is as indifferent to his financial prosperity as he is to the rest of the external world, although the organization that grows up around him is not. Oates never lets us forget what is so attractive about her hero: it is his "intense, hungry, almost greedy look," in which his followers see reflected their own inchoate yearning after meaning, after a way to transcend the spiritual poverty and the confusion of their lives.

At key points in the novel, there are images of

hungry, mangy dogs, reminding us of the opening passages, and images of faulty eyesight, reminding us that Vickery's visions are not to be taken too seriously. Indeed, his visions result from a distorted, almost narcissistic sight, which sees the self as a divinity. In one horrific scene, Vickery, as self-punishment for his lustful thoughts of Leonie, literally plucks out his eye. The scene signifies not only the extraordinary literal way in which the evangelists read the Bible, but also signifies Vickery's incomplete, half-blind vision.

A striking feature of the novel is Oates's deft handling of tone. She does not romanticize Vickery, as she does not romanticize Stephen Petrie and Mered Dawe, and although she makes it clear that Vickery suffers from a disproportionate sense of his own importance, her portrait does not veer toward satire either. She regards him as Milton does Satan, seriously and with some compassion, but also with an acute understanding of his particular brand of hubris. Vickery, "the son of the morning," the name by which Lucifer is addressed in Isaiah, falls from Grace as does Satan, through Pride. His hunger to be special, to overcome his limitations, is manifested in his belief that he is equal to the presence of God.

Vickery's story follows the rhythm of much of Oates's work. She allows her hero or heroine a momentary rise to great romantic heights, only to precipitate his fall back to the ordinary, to necessity, to the demands of time and of history. Thus, at the end of this novel, Oates does not accord Nathan the grace of death. Rather, Nathan Vickery sinks back into anonymity, living in a rented room, seemingly waiting for the "Spirit of the Lord" to return, although he knows it will not. He, like the rest of us, has to live with his hunger, has to live within human limits. The novel stuns and mesmerizes as we are thrown repeatedly from the external world to the insides of Vickery's haunting visions. And like so much of Oates's work, the novel deflates our unreasonable ambitions and dreams in melodramatic and moving prose.

Notes

1. VARIATION ON AN AMERICAN HYMN

1. Robert Phillips, "Joyce Carol Oates: The Art of Fiction," *The Paris Review*, 74 (Fall-Winter 1978), 207–08.
2. Walter Clemons, "Joyce Carol Oates at Home," *New York Times Book Review*, 28 September 1969, p. 4.
3. Respectively, Alfred Kazin, *Bright Book of Life: American Novelists and Storytellers from Hemingway to Mailer* (Boston: Little, Brown, 1974), p. 204; Elizabeth Dalton, quoted in Kazin, p. 199; Brad Darrach, "Consumed by a Piranha Complex," *Life*, 11 December 1970, p. 18.
4. Marvin Mudrick, *The Hudson Review*, 25 (Spring, 1972), 142.
5. S. K. Oberbeck, "A Masterful Explorer in the Minefields of Emotion," *Washington Post Book World*, 17 September 1971, p. 142.
6. Phillips, p. 207.
7. Clemons, p. 48. She spoke of her grandfather at a Trenton State College poetry reading, 13 March 1979.
8. Phillips, pp. 217–18.
9. See Robert H. Fossum's perceptive essay, "Only Control: The Novels of Joyce Carol Oates," *Studies in the Novel*, 7 (Summer 1975), 286.
10. "The Myth of the Isolated Artist," *Psychology Today*, May 1973, p. 75.
11. D. H. Lawrence, *Studies in Classic American Lit-*

erature (1922; rpt. New York: Doubleday, 1953), pp. 85, 152.

12. Richard Poirier, *A World Elsewhere: The Place of Style in American Literature* (New York: Oxford University Press, 1966), p. 5.

13. Ihab Hassan, *Radical Innocence: Studies in the Contemporary American Novel* (Princeton: Princeton University Press, 1961), p. 325.

14. *New Heaven, New Earth: The Visionary Experience In Literature* (New York: Vanguard, 1974), p. 132.

15. *New Heaven, New Earth*, pp. 44–45, 33–35, 45.

16. The raft, the forest, the whaling ship are, of course, references to those quintessential American romances, *Huckleberry Finn, The Scarlet Letter*, and *Moby Dick*.

17. Walter Clemons, "Joyce Carol Oates: Love and Violence," *Newsweek*, 11 December 1972, p. 74.

18. Charles C. Walcutt, *American Literary Naturalism: A Divided Stream* (Minneapolis: University of Minnesota Press, 1956), p. 20.

19. *The Edge of Impossibility: Tragic Forms in Literature* (New York: Vanguard, 1972), pp. 64, 67.

20. *New Heaven, New Earth*, p. 129.

21. From personal notes of an Oates poetry reading at the 92nd Street YMHA, New York City, 10 May 1976.

22. Norman Mailer, "Book Notes," *New York Times Book Review* 14 March 1976.

23. Philip Roth, *Commentary*, 32 (March 1961), 224.

24. Raymond M. Olderman, *Beyond The Waste Land: The American Novel in the Nineteen-Sixties* (New Haven: Yale University Press, 1972), p. 4.

25. Unless otherwise indicated, all quotations are from the first edition of the text, published by Vanguard Press, New York. This story is collected in *The Wheel of Love and Other Stories* (1970).

26. See Joyce M. Wegs, "Don't You Know Who I Am?: The Grotesque in Oates's 'Where Are You Going, Where Have You Been?' " *Journal of Narrative Technique*, 5 (January 1975), 64–72.

27. Poirier, p. 5.
28. Quoted by Richard Chase, *The American Novel and Its Tradition* (New York: Doubleday, 1957), p. 8.
29. *The Literary Criticism of Frank Norris*, Donald Pizer, ed. (Austin: University of Texas Press, 1964), pp. 75–78.
30. Hassan speaks of our culture as an "orgiastic technological fantasy," p. 64.
31. Oates has on several occasions questioned the validity of the fabulators' vision. See "Whose Side Are You On?" *New York Times Book Review*, 4 June 1972, p. 63; "A Personal View of Nabokov," *Saturday Review of the Arts*, 1 (January 1973), 36–37.
32. *Edge of Impossibility*, pp. 14, 16.
33. Letter received from Oates, dated 10 June 1976.
34. See n. 21.
35. Letter received from Oates dated 10 June 1976.
36. *The Wheel of Love and other Stories.*
37. *By the North Gate* (1963) Curiously, there is a Robert Frost poem entitled "The Census Taker." However, Frost regards his census taker with sympathy and not with the deep irony with which Oates regards hers. Nevertheless, Oates's depiction of the landscape in this story suggests Frost's landscape in the poem.
38. Quentin Anderson, *The Imperial Self: An Essay in American Literary and Cultural History* (New York: Knopf, 1971) p. 98.

2.   THE ORDEAL OF INITIATION: *With Shuddering Fall*

1. Leslie Fiedler, *Love and Death in the American Novel*, rev. ed. (New York: Stein and Day, 1966), p. 129.
2. Ihab Hassan, *Radical Innocence: Studies in the Contemporary American Novel* (Princeton: Princeton University Press, 1961), p. 328.
3. Hassan, p. 328.

4. Frederic I. Carpenter, *American Literature and the Dream* (New York: Philosophical Library, 1955), p. 15.
5. Fiedler, p. 129.
6. "Interview with Joyce Carol Oates," *Commonweal* (December 5, 1969), 309.
7. *Advertisements for Myself*, rpt. in *The Long Patrol: 25 Years of Writing from the Work of Norman Mailer*, Robert F. Lucid, ed. (1959; rpt. New York: World Publishing, 1971), pp. 210–11.
8. *Edge of Impossibility: Tragic Forms in Literature* (New York: Vanguard, 1972), p. 11.
9. Shar's sense of communion is similar to the communion felt by Meursault (Camus, *The Stranger*) with the crowd watching his execution.
10. Hassan, p. 44.
11. Letter received from Oates, 19 October 1976.
12. *New Heaven, New Earth: The Visionary Experience in Literature* (New York: Vanguard, 1974), pp. 113–19.

3. WORLD ALIENATION: *A Garden of Earthly Delights*

1. Letter received from Oates, 19 October 1976.
2. *Edge of Impossibility: Tragic Forms in Literature* (New York: Vanguard, 1972), p. 30.
3. See n. 14, Chapter 1.
4. This quotation appears in Granville Hicks, "What is Reality?" *Saturday Review*, 26 October 1968, p. 34.
5. Conversation with Oates, 19 July 1977.
6. Hannah Arendt, *The Human Condition* (Chicago: University of Chicago Press, 1958), p. 256.
7. Arendt, p. 257.
8. See Robert H. Fossum, "Only Control: The Novels of Joyce Carol Oates," *Studies in the Novel*, 7 (Summer 1975), 286.
9. At the poetry reading referred to in n. 21, Chapter 1, Oates declared *Ulysses* the greatest novel ever

written. The novel contains additional literary and mythic allusions. "Swan" not only suggests Dedalus, but Proust's Swann; Clara's family name, Walpole, suggests Horace Walpole; and the town Tintern, of course, suggests Wordsworth's "Lines Written a Few Miles Above Tintern Abbey." See discussion below pp. 50–52.

10. Reference is to the new Modern Library edition (New York, 1961), p. 207.

11. Richard Clark Sterne, "Versions of Rural America," *Nation*, 1 April 1968, p. 450.

12. Page Stegner, "Stone, Berry, Oates—and Other Grist from the Mill," *The Southern Review*, 5 (January 1969), 279.

13. The edition referred to is M. W. Merchant, ed., *Wordsworth: Poetry and Prose* (Cambridge: Harvard University Press, 1955), pp. 152–56.

14. Oates confirmed this in a letter to me, dated 19 October 1976. Stephen A. Shapiro's discussion "The Ambivalent Animal: Man in the Contemporary British and American Novel," *The Centennial Review*, 12 (Winter 1968), 1–22, helped to shape my idea of Swan.

15. Rose Marie Burwell, "Joyce Carol Oates and an Old Master," *Critique: Studies in Modern Fiction*, 15 (1973), 50.

16. See Walter S. Gibson, *Hieronymus Bosch* (New York: Praeger, 1973), p. 50. Gibson, in agreement with other commentators, writes that the painting depicts "mankind as given over to sin" (p. 99). Burwell finds Boschean imagery throughout the novel. I find that it is largely confined to the Swan section in the novel, though Burwell has done Oates readers a service by pointing out the Boschean imagery.

17. Letter received from Oates, dated 19 October 1976.

4.   THE GLUTTONS DREAM
AMERICA: *Expensive People*

1. Louis T. Grant, "A Child of Paradise," *Nation*, 4 November 1968, p. 475.

2. Oates employes this motif in *Wonderland*.
3. Leslie Fiedler, *Love and Death in The American Novel*, rev. ed. (New York: Stein and Day, 1966), pp. 23–38.
4. Bernard Bergonzi, in "Truants," *New York Review of Books*, 2 January 1969, p. 40, writes of *Expensive People*: "Here the mentors seem to be Salinger and Updike and Nabokov. In particular, Miss Oates uses Nabokovian tricks in manipulating the relation of the narrative to ordinary reality."
5. Fiedler, *Waiting for the End* (New York: Stein and Day, 1964), p. 49.
6. Frederic I. Carpenter, *American Literature and the Dream* (New York: Philosophical Library, 1955), p. 6.
7. T. S. Eliot, "The Hollow Men," *Collected Poems, 1909–1962* (New York: Harcourt, Brace, and World, 1963), pp. 81–82.
8. *Edge of Impossibility: Tragic Forms in Literature* (New York: Vanguard, 1972), p. 12.
9. Erich Auerbach, in *Mimesis: The Representation of Reality in Western Literature*, trans. Willard R. Trask (Princeton: Princeton University Press, 1968), p. 137, makes this point about Don Quixote.

5. SHAKESPEARE'S HORATIO
AS THE TYPE
FOR JOYCE CAROL OATES'S
REPRESENTATIVE MAN: *them*

1. Perhaps an exception can be found in *Do With Me What You Will* in which love becomes a means of redemption. Yet it is not romantic love that redeems, but a love stained with crime. See Chapter 7.
2. Elizabeth Janeway, review of *A Garden of Earthly Delights*, *New York Times Book Review*, 10 September 1967, pp. 5, 63.
3. Rose Marie Burwell also argues that the "Swan" section of the novel obviates a naturalistic interpreta-

tion of the book; "Joyce Carol Oates and an Old Master," *Critique: Studies in Modern Fiction*, 15 (1973), 48–49.

4. Ihab Hassan, *Radical Innocence: Studies in the Contemporary American Novel* (Princeton: Princeton University Press, 1961), p. 330.

5. Geoffrey, Wolff, "Gothic City", *Newsweek*, 29 September 1969, p. 120.

6. Guy Davenport, "C'est Magnifique, Mais Ce N'est Pas Daguerre," *Hudson Review*, 23 (Spring 1970), 154–55.

7. *Times Literary Supplement*, 19 March 1971, p. 313.

8. See Georg Lukács, *The Theory of the Novel: A Historico-Philosophical Essay on the Forms of Great Epic Literature*, trans. Anna Bostock (Cambridge: MIT Press, 1971), pp. 56–69, 72.

9. See David Brian Davis, *Homicide in American Fiction, 1798–1860: A Study in Social Values* (Ithaca: Cornell University Press, 1957), p. xiv.

10. See Hannah Arendt, *The Human Condition* (Chicago: University of Chicago Press, 1958), pp. 203–4 and *On Violence* (New York: Harcourt, 1970), pp. 44, 56.

11. James R. Giles, "Suffering, Transcendence, and Artistic 'Form': Joyce Carol Oates's *them*," *Arizona Quarterly*, 32 (Autumn 1976), 216.

12. D. H. Lawrence, *Studies in Classic American Literature* (1923; rpt. New York: Doubleday, 1953), p. 75.

13. Joann Leedom, "Out of Riots—A Quest for Rebirth," *The Christian Science Monitor*, 30 October 1969, p. 12.

14. Jules's conviction that he controls his own fate links him to the rebel Shar of *With Shuddering Fall*, and the conviction that he is his own progenitor links him to the Faustian Kasch of *Childwold*, who finally becomes a prisoner of the world he wanted to recreate.

15. See Mary Allen, *The Necessary Blankness: Women in Major American Fiction of the Sixties* (Urbana:

University of Illinois Press, 1976), for a discussion
of heroines in contemporary fiction with similar
symptoms.

16. An interesting footnote to the discussion of the importance of "names" in Oates's *A Garden of Earthly
Delights* is Maureen's statement, "It is not possible
to escape your name" (408). The statement is a symptom of her return to health.

17. See Arendt, *Human Condition*, p. 237. The passage
in which these ideas are expressed is worth quoting:
"The possible redemption from the predicament of
irreversibility—of being unable to undo what one
has done though one did not, and could not, have
known what he was doing—is the faculty of forgiving. The remedy for unpredictability, for the chaotic
uncertainty of the future, is contained in the faculty
to make and keep promises. The two faculties belong
together in so far as one of them, forgiving, serves
to undo the deeds for the past . . . . and the other,
binding oneself through promises, serves to set up
in the ocean of uncertainty, which the future is by
definition, islands of security without which not
even continuity, let alone durability of any kind,
would be possible in the relationships between
men."

18. Giles, p. 225

19. Leslie Fiedler in *Love and Death in the American
Novel*, rev. ed. (New York: Stein & Day, 1966) states,
"It is maturity above all things that the American
writer fears, and marriage seems to him its essential
sign. For marriage stands traditionally not only for
a reconciliation, but also for a compromise with society, an acceptance of responsibility and drudgery
and dullness," p. 338.

20. Robert M. Adams, "The Best Nightmares are Re-
trospective," *New York Times Book Review*, 28 September 1969, p. 4.

21. In *The New Fiction: Interviews with Innovative
American Writers*, Joe David Bellamy, ed. (Urbana:
University of Illinois Press, 1974), p. 23, Oates

states, "I was very fond of Jules Wendall, the *hero*
of *them* . . ." (emphasis mine).

6. THE JOURNEY FROM THE "I" TO THE "EYE": *Wonderland*

1. In an unpublished paper presented at Special Session 505 of the MLA Convention, 1977, on Joyce Carol Oates's *Wonderland*, Joanne Creighton thoroughly explores the specific analogies between Carroll's Alice books and Oates's *Wonderland.*
2. Personal notes from Oates's class in creative writing, New York University, Summer 1977.
3. See Horace Gregory's "Foreword" to Lewis Carroll, *Alice's Adventures in Wonderland and Through the Looking Glass* (New York: Signet-New American Library, 1960), pp. vii-x.
4. *Times Literary Supplement,* 7 July 1972, p. 765.
5. Leslie Fiedler, *Love and Death in the American Novel,* rev. ed. (New York: Stein and Day, 1966), p. 143.
6. All references are to the Fawcett, paperback edition (Connecticut, 1971); see discussion of variant endings p. 110 and n. 14, Chapter 6.
7. In a perceptive review, Jan B. Gordon argues that *Wonderland* approaches "the loss of history" through the metaphor of "adopted children and their foster parents" just as the Victorians approached this same loss through the metaphor of the orphan. However, Gordon is making clever rather than accurate distinctions. The three elements common to both the Victorian novel and *Wonderland* (Gordon implies as much) in their approach to the "loss of history" are the orphan, his "quest for Origins," and deceiving, rapacious foster parents. *Commonweal,* 11 February 1972, p. 449.
8. Quentin Anderson, *The Imperial Self: An Essay in American Literary and Cultural History* (New York: Knopf, 1971), p. 7.

9. David Brian Davis, *Homocide in American Fiction, 1798–1860: A Study in Social Values* (Ithaca: Cornell University Press, 1957), p. 48.

10. Irving Malin, "The Compulsive Design," *American Dreams, American Nightmares*, David Madden, ed. (Carbondale: Southern Illinois University Press, 1970), p. 58.

11. Calvin Bedient's very wise review entitled "Blind Mouths" makes the point that "To eat others to feed identity, to spew them out to escape it—the book roils with the futile strain of both." *Partisan Review*, 39 (Winter 1972), 124.

12. Roquentin: "I draw my face closer until it touches the mirror. The eyes, nose and mouth disappear: nothing human is left. Brown wrinkles show on each side of the feverish swelled lips, crevices, mole holes. A silky white down covers the great slopes of the cheeks, two hairs protrude from the nostrils: It is a geological embossed map." Jean Paul Sartre, *Nausea*, trans. Lloyd Alexander (New York: New Directions, 1964), p. 17.

13. *Wonderland*, 1st ed. (New York: Vangaurd, 1971), p. 512.

14. Oates reports that the Fawcett edition is the one she prefers in *American Journal*, 3 July 1973, pp. 17–21.

15. See Anderson, p. 54. In his study of nineteenth-century writers, Anderson comes to a similar conclusion, associating extreme individualism with an infantile narcissism.

16. Walter Clemons, "Joyce Carol Oates at Home," *New York Times Book Review*, 28 September 1969, p. 48.

17. Joe David Bellamy, ed. *The New Fiction: Interviews with Innovative American Writers* (Urbana: University of Illinois Press, 1974), p. 23.

7. CRIME-CROSSED LOVERS:
Do With Me What You Will

1. See Sigmund Freud, "On Narcissism: An Introduction," in Vol. 4 of *Collected Papers of Sigmund Freud* (New York: Basic Books, 1959), p. 31.

2. Norman O. Brown summarizes this Freudian point: "At the mother's breast, in Freudian language, the child experiences that primal condition, forever after idealized, 'in which object-libido and ego-libido cannot be distinguished'." *Life Against Death: The Psychoanalytic Meaning of History* (Connecticut: Wesleyan University Press, 1959), p. 51.

3. *New Heaven, New Earth: The Visionary Experience in Literature* (New York: Vanguard, 1974), p. 132.

4. Sara Sanborn, in her review of the novel, notes the fairy-tale element. "Two Major Novelists All by Herself," *Nation*, January 1974, p. 20.

5. That, in the course of the novel, Elena reads *Middlemarch* suggests some affinities between George Eliot's work and Oates's. The marriage contract, for instance, is suggestive of the cold, formal letter in which Casaubon proposes marriage to Dorothea. In addition, after Casaubon's death, Dorothea defies the dictates of Casaubon's will by marrying Will Ladislaw, whom she loves. Similarly, Elena defies her marriage contract by running away with Jack Morrissey.

6. In speaking about the novel at a special session on her works, Oates said their love is "fated," that they cannot help themselves. Special Session 17: The Fiction of Joyce Carol Oates, MLA Convention, New York, 26 December 1976.

7. "The Myth of the Isolated Artist," *Psychology Today*, May 1973, p. 75.

8. Ibid.

9. This essay is collected in *New Heaven and New Earth*, pp. 118–19.

10. Freud, p. 42.

11. Freud, p. 32.

12. Bernard Bailyn, *The Ideological Origins of the American Revolution* (Cambridge: Harvard University Press, 1967), p. 182.

13. Bailyn, p. 20.

14. *New Heaven, New Earth*, p. 124.

15. Freud, p. 46.

16. "The Hostile Sun: The Poetry of D. H. Lawrence," collected in *New Heaven, New Earth*, p. 47.

17. No doubt, this is Oates's jab at Sylvia Plath whose novel is entitled *The Bell Jar*.
18. For additional examples of Elena's self-objectification see *Do With Me What You Will*, pp. 118, 380.
19. Constance Ayers Denne makes the point that "Like the symbolic act of Adam and Eve in the Christian myth, this too is a criminal act, an act of self-assertion which shatters the old paternalistic structures." "Joyce Carol Oates's Women," *Nation*, December 1974, p. 599.
20. Freud, p. 59.
21. In a *Library Journal* interview, Oates reveals that the prototype for Dawe is a member of the White Panthers who was sentenced to fifteen years for possessing a marijuana cigarette. John Alfred Avant, "An Interview with Joyce Carol Oates," 15 November 1972, p. 3711.
22. In James Gould Cozzens' novel, *By Love Possessed* (New York: Harcourt, 1957), the central character, a lawyer and an archetypal righteous man, chooses to commit a crime rather than betray a friend. He, too, pleads *nolo contendere*. See p. 554.

8. TOWARD PLURALISM: *The Assassins:*
A Book of Hours

1. William James, *Varieties of Religious Experience: A Study of Human Nature, Being. The Gifford Lectures on Natural Religion Delivered at Edinburgh in 1901–1902* (1902; rpt. New York: Modern Library, 1936).
2. William James, "Dilemma of Determinism," *The Will to Believe and Other Essays in Popular Philosophy and Human Immortality* (1896; rpt. New York: Dover, 1956), pp. 179–80.
3. The directions explored in this chapter were suggested in a conversation I had with Ms. Oates on 19 July 1977 at New York University where she was teaching a course in creative writing.

4. Sacvan Bercovitch in his "Introduction" to *The American Puritan Imagination: Essays in Revaluation* (New York: Cambridge University Press, 1974) gives an excellent summary of the Puritan's sense of divine errand. See especially pp. 7–10.

5. In a letter to me dated June 10, 1976, Oates wrote of *The Assassins:* "The desire for absolute control is an infantile fantasy; delusions of omnipotence are indicative of mental illness. The parallel with American aspirations in the twentieth-century is obvious, but I didn't intend to write allegorical novels—subordinating the individual to the collective doesn't interest me."

6. F. H. Sandbach, *The Stoics* (New York: Norton, 1975), pp. 50–51.

7. In my conversation with Ms. Oates (see n. 3, Chapter 8), she declared that William James is her favorite American author, though Oates directly incorporates James's philosophy in her fiction for the first time in this book. In her essay on Troilus and Cressida, she refers to William James (*Edge of Impossibility*, p. 19).

8. For an account of the James's family history, I relied on the very readable *William James: A Biography* by Gay Wilson Allen (New York: Viking Press, 1967).

9. Allen, pp. 505–07.

10. William James, "A Pluralistic Universe," *Essays in Radical Empiricism and A Pluralistic Universe*, ed. Ralph Barton Perry (1909 and 1912; rpt. New York: Dutton, 1971), pp. 273–75.

11. *New Heaven, New Earth: The Visionary Experience in Literature* (New York: Vanguard, 1974), p. 244.

12. "A Pluralistic Universe," p. 184.

13. *New Heaven, New Earth,* pp. 259–60.

14. "A Pluralistic Universe," p. 270.

15. "A Pluralistic Universe," p. 177.

16. William James, Lecture II of *Pragmatism: A New Name for Some Old Ways of Thinking* (New York: Longmans, Green, and Co., 1907), p. 45.

17.   For instance, Michael G. Cooke, "Recent Novels: Woman bearing Violence," *The Yale Review* 66 (October 1976), 148–50.

18.   See Albert Einstein and Leopold Infield, *The Evolution of Physics; The Growth of Ideas from Early Concepts to Relativity and Quanta* (New York: Simon and Schuster, 1938), pp. 160–260.

19.   Curiously, in his preface to *The Will to Believe*, James anticipates the perceptions of modern physics. "To the very last, there are the various 'points of view' which the philosopher must distinguish in discussing the world; and what is inwardly clear from one point remains a bare externality and datum to the other . . . . There is no possible point of view from which the world can appear an absolutely single fact" (pp. viii-ix). What James did not anticipate, however, is that the very physical laws governing the universe are as impenetrable to absolute definition as are metaphysical truths.

20.   Oates has probably modelled Hugh on George Grosz and James Gillray, whose names Hugh invokes. George Grosz was a twentieth-century German caricaturist who rose to fame with his savage, antiestablishment sketches, and who in later life moved to America. According to a biographer, Hans Hess, "He was convinced of the incorrigible, unalterable, evil stupidity of men," and at the end "he believed in nothing except money and success," convictions Hugh also holds. James Gillray, an eighteenth-century English cartoonist who often satirized George III, was, like Hugh, an impoverished alcoholic who finally attempted suicide. *George Grosz* (New York: Macmillan, 1974), p. 179 and Draper Hill, *Mr. Gillray, The Caricaturist* (London: Phaidon Press, 1965), pp. 142–52.

21.   "A Personal View of Nabokov," *Saturday Review of the Arts* (January 1973), 37.

22.   Andrew's journal is probably named for Hume's *Political Discourses*. Andrew's empirical philosophy resembles Hume's more than it does James's, in that

it is deeply skeptical. But it is merely a surface re-
semblance because Andrew's ideas as they are fil-
tered through Yvonne are confused and as she comes
to realize, contradictory, a word empire that ignores
the phenomenological world.

23. See "Conclusions" and "Postscript," *Varieties,* pp. 485–527.

24. *The New Republic,* 2 July 1977, pp. 36–37.

25. See Lecture XI, "Conversion," *Varieties,* pp. 186–253, in which James gives accounts of several conversion dreams. One dream is experienced by a man named Stephen (H. Bradley).

26. "A Pluralistic Universe," p. 142.

27. It includes the famous aphorism *tat tvam asi* (that art thou) from the Chāndogya Upanishad, as well as transformed Sanskirt words: The source for "kick-shawsees" is probably *caksusa,* meaning something like "divine eyesight"; and "pruta" is probably de-rived from *preta,* indicating the "hungry ghosts" shown in lower segments of the Tibetan Wheel of Life. (Significantly, Oates has a volume of short sto-ries entitled *Hungry Ghosts.*) This is the purgatory where men between lives are tortured by their own unsatisfied desires.

28. *New Heaven, New Earth,* p. 50. Generally, Oates's criticism of other writers is revelatory of her own work.

29. D. H. Lawrence, *Studies in Classic American Lit-erature* (1923; rpt. New York: Doubleday, 1953), p. 124.

9. THE VICTORY OF EROS: *Childwold*

1. William James, "A Pluralistic Universe," *Essays in Radical Empiricism and A Pluralistic Universe,* ed. Ralph Barton Perry (1909 and 1912; rpt. New York: Dutton, 1971), pp. 164–65.

2. In *Beyond the Pleasure Principle* (London: Hogarth Press, 1930); rpt. in *The Major Works of Sigmund*

Freud, Great Books of the Western World, ed. Robert M. Hutchins, vol. 57 (Chicago: Encyclopedia Britannica, 1952), pp. 658–59, Freud equates the ego instincts with the death instincts and the sexual instincts with the life instincts. Oates seems to be making similar equations in her fiction.

3. Vale does not live with his mother, but he is, after all, an adult.

4. *Marriages and Infidelities* (1972); in a brilliant article, "Autonomy and Influence: Joyce Carol Oates's *Marriages and Infidelities,*" Eileen Bender investigates these Oatesian revisions. Bender's argument is that Oates "suggests a radical revision of the image of the artist, a refutation of 'the myth of the isolated artist,' a vision of a cultural continuum of shared created effort . . . ." By contrasting Oates's sense of herself as an artist working a cultural context with fabulators' "autonomous" art, Bender reaches conclusions about Oates's vision that are similar to mine. *Soundings,* 58 (1975), 390–406; the quotation appears on p. 393.

5. "Whose Side Are You On?" *New York Times Book Review,* 4 June 1972, p. 63.

6. *New Heaven, New Earth: The Visionary Experience in Literature* (New York: Vanguard Press, 1974), p. 127.

7. Humbert calls Lolita his "own creation," having "no will, no consciousness—indeed no life of her own." Indeed, Kasch and Humbert both call their nymphs "Lilith." Vladimir Nabokov, *Lolita* (New York: Olympia Press, 1955), pp. 64, 21.

8. Henry David Thoreau, "Where I Lived, and What I Live For," *Walden; or, Life in the Woods* (1854; rpt. New York: New American Library, 1942), p. 66. The passage Oates echoes is: "I went to the woods because I wished to live deliberately, to front only the essential facts of life . . . . I wanted to live deep and suck out all the marrow of life, to live so sturdily and Spartan-like as to rout all that was not life, to cut a broad swath and shave close, to drive life into a

corner, and reduce it to its lowest terms . . . ." Thoreau's purpose is close to Kasch's in that he wishes to reduce the manifold. Curiously, Oates has written a short piece for *Mademoiselle*, praising Thoreau, in which she cites this quotation. What she praises, however, is Thoreau's appreciation of nature and his ability to bring "into ordinary day-to-day experience" the "transcendental vision." But by putting this quotation in the mouth of Kasch, she gives it an altered context; "Joyce Carol Oates on Thoreau's *Walden*," *Mademoiselle*, April 1973, pp. 96–98. Also see p. 157 in the novel for an additional allusion to Thoreau.

9. This quotation is from Bruce Wilshire, who wrote the introduction to *William James: The Essential Writing*, ed. Bruce Wilshire (New York: Harper and Row, 1971), p. xxxiv.

10. "A Pluralistic Universe," p. 247.

11. Alfred Aspel, Jr., "Lolita: The Springboard of Parody" in *Nabokov: The Man and His World*, ed. L. S. Dembo (Madison: University of Wisconsin Press, 1967), p. 111.

12. "A Pluralistic Universe," p. 243.

13. Oates is making very clever use of the theory of the recapitulation of ontogeny by phylogeny. As defined by Carl Sagan, in *The Dragons of Eden: Speculations on the Evolution of Human Intelligence* (New York: Random House, 1977), pp. 255, 257–58, this theory proposes that there is a "repetition, during the embryonic development of an individual organism, of a past evolutionary stage of the species." This theory was advanced by Ernst Haeckel, a nineteenth-century German anatomist, who "held that in its embryological development, an animal tends to repeat or recapitulate the sequence that its ancestors followed during their evolution." Kasch mentions the name of Garstung, who not only wrote scientific treatises on the theory of "paedomorphosis" but poems as well. Garstung's theories are discussed

in Stephen Jay Gould's *Ontogeny and Phylogeny* (Cambridge: Harvard University Press, 1977).

14. Quentin Anderson, *The Imperial Self: An Essay in American Literary and Cultural History* (New York: Knopf, 1971), p. 36.

15. See my discussion below, pp. 184–85.

16. "The Children" is collected in *Marriages and Infidelities.*

17. The philosophic analogue to this may be found in James's statement that "Reality *falls* in passing into conceptual analysis; it *mounts* in living its own undivided life—it buds and burgeons, changes and creates . . . . Philosophy should seek this kind of living understanding of the movement of reality, not follow science in vainly patching together forgotten fragments of its dead results," *Essays in Radical Empiricism and A Pluralistic Universe,* p. 248.

10. EPILOGUE

1. Frank Budgen, *James Joyce and the Making of Ulysses* (Bloomington: Indiana University Press, 1960), pp. 15–16.

2. "The Myth of the Isolated Artist," *Psychology Today,* May 1973, p. 75. Though the emphasis is different, Oates's argument is similar to that of T. S. Eliot in "Tradition and the Individual Talent." See *Selected Prose of T. S. Eliot.* (New York: Harcourt, 1975). Also see Bender, "Autonomy and Influence," to whom I am indebted for this point; *Soundings,* 58 (Fall 1975), 390–406.

3. Henry James, *The Golden Bowl* (1904; rpt. New York: Penguin, 1973), p. 9.

Bibliography

Works by Joyce Carol Oates

Novels

The Assassins: A Book of Hours. New York: Vanguard, 1975.

Childwold. New York: Vanguard, 1976.

Do With Me What You Will. New York: Vanguard, 1973.

Expensive People. New York: Vanguard, 1968.

A Garden of Earthly Delights. New York: Vanguard, 1967.

Son of the Morning. New York: Vanguard, 1978.

them. New York: Vanguard, 1969.

With Shuddering Fall. New York: Vanguard, 1964.

Wonderland. New York: Vanguard, 1971.

Wonderland. Greenwich, Connecticut: Fawcett, 1973.

Short Stories

All the Good People I've Left Behind. Santa Barbara: Black Sparrow Press, 1979.

By the North Gate. New York: Vanguard, 1963.

Crossing the Border: Fifteen Tales. New York: Vanguard, 1976.

The Goddess and Other Women. New York: Vanguard, 1974.

The Hungry Ghosts: Seven Allusive Comedies. Los Angeles: Black Sparrow Press, 1974.

Marriages and Infidelities. New York: Vanguard, 1972.

Night-Side: Eighteen Tales. New York: Vanguard, 1977.

The Poisoned Kiss and Other Stories. New York: Vanguard, 1975.

Scenes From American Life: Contemporary Short Fiction. ed. Joyce Carol Oates. New York: Random House, 1972.

The Seduction and Other Stories. Los Angeles: Black Sparrow Press, 1975.

Upon the Sweeping Flood. New York: Vanguard, 1966.

The Wheel of Love and Other Stories. New York: Vanguard, 1970.

Where Are You Going, Where Have You Been?: Stories of Young America. Greenwich, Connecticut: Fawcett, 1974.

Novella

The Triumph of the Spider Monkey: The First Person Confession of the Maniac Bobby Gotteson as Told to Joyce Carol Oates. Santa Barbara: Black Sparrow Press, 1976.

Poetry

Angel Fire. Baton Rouge: Louisiana State University Press, 1973.

Anonymous Sins and Other Poems. Baton Rouge: Louisiana State University Press, 1969.

Dreaming America. n. p.: Aloe Editions, 1973.

The Fabulous Beasts. Baton Rouge: Louisiana State University Press, 1975.

Love and Its Derangements and Other Poems. Baton Rouge: Louisiana State University Press, 1970.

Season of Peril. Santa Barbara: Black Sparrow Press, 1977.

Women in Love and Other Poems. New York: Albondacani Press, 1968.

Women Whose Lives Are Food, Men Whose Lives Are Money. Baton Rouge: Louisiana State University Press, 1978.

Plays

Miracle Play. Los Angeles: Black Sparrow Press, 1974.
"Ontological Proof of My Existence." *Partisan Review*,
37 (1970), 471–97.

Criticism

"Art: Therapy and Magic." *American Journal*, 3 (July
1973), 17–21.
"Background and Foreground in Fiction." *Writer*, 80
(August 1967), 11–13.
"Building Tension in the Short Story." *Writer*, 78 (June
1966), 11–12.
The Edge of Impossibility: Tragic Forms in Literature.
New York: Vanguard, 1972.
The Hostile Sun: The Poetry of D. H. Lawrence. Los An-
geles: Black Sparrow Press, 1973.
"Joyce Carol Oates on Thoreau's *Walden*." Mademoi-
selle, April 1973, pp. 96–98.
"The Myth of the Isolated Artist." *Psychology Today*,
May 1973, pp. 74–75.
*New Heaven, New Earth: The Visionary Experience in
Literature*. New York: Vanguard, 1974.
"A Personal View of Nabokov." *Saturday Review of the
Arts*, 1 (January 1973), 36–37.
Review of *The Simone Weil Reader*. *The New Republic*,
2 July 1977, pp. 33–37.
"Unique/Universal in Fiction." *Writer*, 86 (January 1973),
9–12.
"Updike's American Comedies." *Modern Fiction Stud-
ies*, 21 (Autumn 1972), 459–72.
"A Visit with Doris Lessing." *Southern Review*, 9 (Au-
tumn 1973), 873–82.
"Whose Side Are You On?" *New York Times Book Re-
view*, 4 June 1972, p. 63.

WORKS ON JOYCE CAROL OATES

Allen, Mary. *The Necessary Blankness: Women in Major
American Fiction of the Sixties*. Urbana: University
of Illinois Press, 1976.

Andersen, Sally. "The Poetry of Joyce Carol Oates."
    Spirit, 39 (1972), 24–29.
Avant, John Alfred. "An Interview with Joyce Carol
    Oates." *Library Journal*, 15 November 1972, pp.
    3711–12.
Bedient, Calvin. "Blind Mouths." *Partisan Review*, 39
    (Winter 1972), 124–27.
Bellamy, Joe David, ed. "Joyce Carol Oates." *The New
    Fiction: Interviews with Innovative American Writ-
    ers*. Urbana: University of Illinois Press, 1974, pp.
    19–31.
Bender, Eileen T. " 'Assault of Hope': The Artistic Vision,
    Theory and Practice of Joyce Carol Oates." Diss.
    University of Notre Dame, 1977.
———. "Autonomy and Influence: Joyce Carol Oates's
    Marriages and Infidelities." *Soundings*, 58 (1975),
    390–406.
Bergonzi, Bernard. "Truants." *New York Review of
    Books*, 2 January 1969, p. 40.
Bower, W. "Bliss in the First Person." *Saturday Review*,
    26 October 1968, pp. 34–35.
Burwell, Rose Marie. "Joyce Carol Oates and an Old
    Master." *Critique*, 15 (1973), 48–58.
———. "The Process of Individuation as Narrative Struc-
    ture: Joyce Carol Oates's *Do With Me What You
    Will*." *Critique*, 17 (1975), 93–106.
Catron, Douglas M. "A Contribution to a Bibliography of
    Works by and about Joyce Carol Oates." *American
    Literature*, 49 (1977), 399–414.
Clemons, Walter. "Joyce Carol Oates at Home." *New
    York Times Book Review*, 28 September 1969, pp. 4,
    48.
———. "Joyce Carol Oates: Love and Violence." *News-
    week*, 11 December 1972, p. 74.
Cooke, Michael G. "Recent Novels: Women Bearing
    Violence." *The Yale Review*, 66 (October 1976), 148,
    150.
Creighton, Joanne V. *Joyce Carol Oates*. Boston: G. K.
    Hall, 1979.
———. "Joyce Carol Oates's Craftsmanship in *The Wheel*

of Love." *Studies in Short Fiction*, 15 (Fall 1978), 375–84.

———. "Unliberated Women in Joyce Carol Oates's Fiction." *World Literature Written in English*, 17 (April 1978), 165–75.

Dalton, Elizabeth. "Joyce Carol Oates: Violence in the Head." *Commentary*, 49 (June 1970), 75.

Darrach, Brad. "Consumed by a Piranha Complex." *Life*, 11 December 1970, p. 18.

Davenport, Guy. "C'est Magnifique, Mais Ce N'est Pas Daguerre." *Hudson Review*, 23 (Spring 1970), 154.

Denne, Constance Ayers. "Joyce Carol Oates's Women." *Nation*, December 1974, pp. 597–99.

Ditsky, John. "The Man on the Quaker Oats Box: Characteristics of Recent Experimental Fiction." *Georgia Review*, 26 (Fall 1972), 297–313.

Fossum, R. H. "Only Control: The Novels of Joyce Carol Oates." *Studies in the Novel*, 7 (Summer 1975), 285–97.

Giles, James R. "The 'Marivaudian Being' Drowns His Children: Dehumanization in Donald Barthelme's 'Robert Kennedy Saved from Drowning' and Joyce Carol Oates's *Wonderland*." *Southern Humanities Review*, 9 (1975), 63–75.

———. "Suffering, Transcendence, and Artistic 'Form': Joyce Carol Oates's *them*." *Arizona Quarterly*, 32 (Autumn 1976), 213–26.

Godwin, Gail. "An Oates Scrapbook." *North American Review*, 256 (Winter 1971), 76–80.

Gordon, Jan B. "Gothic Fiction and the Losing Battle to Contain Oneself." *Commonweal*, 11 February 1972, p. 449.

Grant, Louis T. "A Child of Paradise." *Nation*, November 1968, p. 475.

Grant, Mary Kathryn. *The Tragic Vision of Joyce Carol Oates*. Durham, North Carolina: Duke University Press, 1978.

Hodge, Marion Cecil, Jr. "What Moment is not Terrible? An Introduction to the Work of Joyce Carol Oates." Diss. University of Tennessee, 1974.

Janeway, Elizabeth. Review of *A Garden of Earthly Delights*. *New York Times Book Review*, 10 September 1967, pp. 5, 63.

Kazin, Alfred. *Bright Book of Life: American Novelists and Storytellers from Hemingway to Mailer*. Boston: Little, Brown, 1974.

Kuehl, Linda. "Interview with Joyce Carol Oates," *Commonweal*, 5 December 1969, 307–10.

Leedom, Joann. "Out of the Riots—A Quest for Rebirth." *Christian Science Monitor*, 30 October 1969, p. 12.

Martin, Alice Conkright. "Toward a Higher Consciousness: A Study of the Novels of Joyce Carol Oates." Diss. Northern Illinois University, 1974.

McCormick, Lucienne P. "A Bibliography of Works by and about Joyce Carol Oates." *American Literature*, 43 (1971), 124–32.

Mudrick, Marvin. "Fiction and Truth." *Hudson Review*, 25 (Spring 1972), 142.

Oberbeck, S. K. "A Masterful Explorer in the Minefields of Emotion." *Washington Post Book World*, 17 September 1972, 10.

Petite, Joseph. "The Interrelatedness of Marriage, Passion, and Female Identity in the Fiction of Joyce Carol Oates." Diss. Kansas State University, 1976.

Phillips, Robert. "Joyce Carol Oates: The Art of Fiction." *The Paris Review* 74 (Fall-Winter 1978), 199–226.

Pickering, S. F., Jr. "The Short Stories of Joyce Carol Oates." *Georgia Review*, 28 (Summer 1974), 218–26.

Prescott, Peter S. "Everyday Monsters." *Newsweek*, 11 October 1971, p. 96.

Ricks, Christopher. "The Unignorable Real." *New York Review of Books*, 12 February 1970, pp. 22–24.

Sanborn, Sara. "Two Major Novelists All By Herself." *Nation*, January 1974, p. 20.

Spacks, Patricia Meyer. "A Chronicle of Women." *Hudson Review*, 25 (Spring 1972), 168.

Stegner, Page. "Stone, Berry, Oates—And Other Grist from the Mill." *Southern Review*, 5 (January 1969), 273–301.

Sterne, Richard Clarke, "Versions of Rural America." *Nation*, 1 April 1968, p. 450.

Stevens, Cynthia Charlotte. "The Imprisoned Imagination: The Family in the Fiction of Joyce Carol Oates, 1960–1970." Diss. University of Illinois at Urbana, 1974.

Sullivan, Walter, "Old Age, Death, and Other Modern Landscapes: Good and Indifferent Fables for our Times." *Sewanee Review*, 82 (1974), 138–47.

Taylor, Gordon O. "Joyce Carol Oates: Artist in *Wonderland*." *Southern Review*, 10 (1974), 490–503.

Times Literary Supplement, Review of *them*. 19 March 1971, p. 313.

Times Literary Supplement, Review of *Wonderland*. 7 July 1972, p. 765.

Wagner, Linda W. ed. *Joyce Carol Oates: The Critical Reception*. Boston: G. K. Hall, 1979.

Walker, Carolyn. "Fear, Love, and Art in Oates's 'Plot.'" *Critique*, 15 (1973), 59–70.

Waller, G. F. "Joyce Carol Oates's *Wonderland:* An Introduction." *Dalhousie Review*, 54 (1974), 480–90.

———. *Dreaming America: Obsession and Transcendence in the Fiction of Joyce Carol Oates*. Baton Rouge: Louisiana State University Press, 1979.

Wegs, Joyce, M. "The Grotesque in Some American Novels of the 1960s.: Ken Kesey, Joyce Carol Oates, Sylvia Plath." Diss. University of Illinois at Urbana, 1974.

———. "Don't You Know Who I Am?: The Grotesque in Oates's 'Where Are You Going, Where Have You Been?' " *Journal of Narrative Technique*, 5 (January 1975), 64–72.

Wolff, Geoffrey. "Gothic City." *Newsweek*, 29 September 1969, p. 120.

Author Index

227